JAMESTOWN  PUBLISHERS

Themes *in*
Reading

VOLUME ③

A MULTICULTURAL COLLECTION

JAMESTOWN  PUBLISHERS
A DIVISION OF NTC/CONTEMPORARY
PUBLISHING COMPANY

Manufactured in the United States of America
International Standard Book Number: 0-89061-813-5
10 9 8 7 6 5 4 3 2 1

Executive Editor
Marilyn Cunningham

Editorial
Michael Carpenter
Paulinda Lynk
Bernice Rappoport

Permissions
Doris Milligan

Production and Design
PiperStudiosInc

Illustrations
Jason O'Malley

Contents

Unit 1: Expressions of Love

Unit 2: Special People

Unit 3: Food for Thought

Unit 4: American History

Expressions
of Love

Love is a powerful emotion. We learn how to love
from other people who love us. We learn from their
expressions of love: a parent soothes a sick child,
an older sister gives a favorite game to her brother,
or a friend listens when another friend needs to talk.
These are some everyday expressions of love.

In this unit you will read about people who love each
other. They express their love in different ways, and
sometimes they do not know how to express it.
Some expressions of love are ordinary, everyday
actions. Others involve major sacrifices.

As you read, think about the people that you love
and those that love you. Why do you love them? Why
do they love you? How do you express your love for
them? How do they show that they love you?

When I Hear Your Name

Gloria Fuertes

When I hear your name
I feel a little robbed of it;
it seems unbelievable
that half a dozen letters could say so much.

My compulsion[1] is to blast down every wall with
    your name,
I'd paint it on all the houses,
there wouldn't be a well
I hadn't leaned into
to shout your name there,
nor a stone mountain
where I hadn't uttered[2]
those six separate letters
that are echoed back.

My compulsion is
to teach the birds to sing it,
to teach the fish to drink it,
to teach men that there is nothing
like the madness of repeating your name.

The speaker in this poem can't get someone's name out of her mind. What does that tell about her feelings?

[1] uncontrollable impulse or desire

[2] spoken

My compulsion is to forget altogether
the other 22 letters, all the numbers,
the books I've read, the poems I've written.
To say hello with your name.
To beg bread with your name.
'She always says the same thing,' they'd say when
    they saw me,
and I'd be so proud, so happy, so self-contained.

And I'll go to the other world with your name on my
    tongue,
and all their questions I'll answer with your name—
the judges and saints will understand nothing—
God will sentence me to repeating it endlessly and
    forever.

About the Author

Gloria Fuertes is well known in Spain, not only for her poetry but also for her children's stories. About fifteen years of her writing career were spent writing stories for children's magazines. Ms. Fuertes, known for her humor and compassion, has also presented poetry readings and recorded many of her poems.

Responding to the Poem

▼ Think Back

Which statements in the poem are exaggerations?

At the end of the poem, the speaker imagines being sentenced by God to repeat the special person's name "endlessly and forever." Does the speaker fear or welcome that sentence? How can you tell?

▼ Discuss

We are told how the speaker feels when hearing the name of a special person, but we are never told what the name is. Why might the poet have chosen not to give it?

What do you think the speaker means by the statement "When I hear your name/I feel a little robbed of it"?

Is "When I Hear Your Name" a love poem? Why or why not? If it isn't a love poem, what other emotion might the speaker be feeling? Explain.

▼ Write

Create Sound Images The imagery in "When I Hear Your Name" appeals mostly to the sense of sound. Reread the poem to identify sound imagery. Can you create other sound images that could be part of the poem?

Write a Poem Is there someone you really like or dislike? Write a poem that explains how you feel. Build your poem around imagery that appeals to one of the senses. Begin by finishing the statement: "When I hear your name, I . . ."

The Good Stuff

Robert Fulghum

T he cardboard box is marked "The Good Stuff." As I write, I can see the box where it is stored on a high shelf in my studio.¹ I like being able to see it when I look up. The box contains those odds and ends of personal treasures that have survived many bouts² of clean-it-out-and-throw-it-away that seize me from time to time. The box has passed through the screening done as I've moved from house to house and hauled stuff from attic to attic. A thief looking into the box would not take anything—he couldn't get a dime for any of it. But if the house ever catches on fire, the box goes with me when I run.

One of the keepsakes in the box is a small paper bag. Lunch size. Though the top is sealed with duct tape, staples, and several paper clips, there is a ragged rip in one side through which the contents may be seen.

This particular lunch sack has been in my care for maybe fourteen years. But it really belongs to my daughter, Molly. Soon after she came of school age, she

We all save things that are important to us. What is the thing that Robert Fulghum can't bear to throw away?

¹ place where a writer, artist, or other craftsperson works

² rounds; times

became an enthusiastic participant in packing the morning lunches for herself, her brothers, and me. Each bag got a share of sandwiches, apples, milk money, and sometimes a note or a treat. One morning Molly handed me two bags as I was about to leave. One regular sack. And the one with the duct tape and staples and paper clips. "Why two bags?" "The other one is something else." "What's in it?" "Just some stuff—take it with you." Not wanting to hold court over the matter, I stuffed both sacks into my briefcase, kissed the child, and rushed off.

At midday, while hurriedly scarfing down my real lunch, I tore open Molly's bag and shook out the contents. Two hair ribbons, three small stones, a plastic dinosaur, a pencil stub, a tiny seashell, two animal crackers, a marble, a used lipstick, a small doll, two chocolate kisses, and thirteen pennies.

I smiled. How charming. Rising to hustle off to all the important business of the afternoon, I swept the desk clean—into the wastebasket—leftover lunch, Molly's junk, and all. There wasn't anything in there I needed.

That evening Molly came to stand beside me while I was reading the paper. "Where's my bag?" "What bag?" "You know, the one I gave you this morning." "I left it at the office, why?" "I forgot to put this note in it." She hands over the note. "Besides, I want it back?" "Why?" "Those are my things in the sack, Daddy, the ones I really like—I thought you might like to play with them, but now I want them back. You didn't lose the bag, did you, Daddy?" Tears puddled in her eyes. "Oh no, I just forgot to bring it home," I lied. "Bring it tomorrow, okay?" "Sure thing—don't worry." As she hugged my neck with relief, I unfolded the note that had not got into the sack: "I love you, Daddy."

Oh.

And also—uh-oh.

I looked long at the face of my child.

She was right—what was in that sack was "something else."

Molly had given me her treasures. All that a seven-year-old held dear. Love in a paper sack. And I had missed it. Not only missed it, but had thrown it in the wastebasket because "there wasn't anything in there I needed." Dear God.

It wasn't the first or the last time I felt my Daddy Permit was about to run out.

It was a long trip back to the office. But there was nothing else to be done. So I went. The pilgrimage[3] of a penitent.[4] Just ahead of the janitor, I picked up the wastebasket and poured the contents on my desk. I was sorting it all out when the janitor came in to do his chores. "Lose something?" "Yeah, my mind." "It's probably in there, all right. What's it look like and I'll help you find it?" I started not to tell him. But I couldn't feel any more of a fool than I was already in fact, so I told him. He didn't laugh. He smiled. "I got kids, too." So the brotherhood of fools searched the trash and found the jewels and he smiled at me and I smiled at him. You are never alone in these things. Never.

[3] journey

[4] one who is sorry for his or her sins

After washing the mustard off the dinosaurs and spraying the whole thing with breath-freshener to kill the smell of onions, I carefully smoothed out the wadded ball of brown paper into a semifunctional[5] bag and put the treasures inside and carried the whole thing home gingerly,[6] like an injured kitten. The next evening I returned it to Molly, no questions asked, no explanations offered. The bag didn't look so good, but the stuff was all there and that's what counted. After dinner I asked her to tell me about the stuff in the sack, and so she took it all out a piece at a time and placed the objects in a row on the dining room table.

It took a long time to tell. Everything had a story, a memory, or was attached to dreams and imaginary friends. Fairies had brought some of the things. And I had given her the chocolate kisses, and she had kept them for when she needed them. I managed to say, "I see" very wisely several times in the telling. And as a matter of fact, I did see.

To my surprise, Molly gave the bag to me once again several days later. Same ratty bag. Same stuff inside. I felt forgiven. And trusted. And loved. And a little more comfortable wearing the title of Father. Over several months the bag went with me from time to time. It was never clear to me why I did or did not get it on a given day. I began to think of it as the Daddy Prize and tried to be good the night before so I might be given it the next morning.

In time Molly turned her attention to other things . . . found other treasures . . . lost interest in the game . . . grew up. Something. Me? I was left holding the bag. She gave it to me one morning and never asked for its return. And so I have it still.

Sometimes I think of all the times in this sweet life when I must have missed the affection I was being given. A friend calls this "standing knee-deep in the river and dying of thirst."

So the worn paper sack is there in the box. Left over from a time when a child said, "Here—this is the best I've got. Take it—it's yours. Such as I have, give I to thee."

I missed it the first time. But it's my bag now.

About the Author

Robert Fulghum was born in Waco, Texas, in 1937. He is a painter, writer, and lecturer who has also had careers as a part-time minister and as an art teacher. Unlike some writers who struggle for years, Fulghum had immediate success with his first book, *All I Really Need to Know I Learned in Kindergarten*. The themes of his essays touch readers with their simplicity, humor, and insight into human nature. "The Good Stuff" is from his 1988 book *It Was on Fire When I Lay Down On It*.

Responding to the Essay

▼ Think Back

What meaning did the items in the bag have for Molly?

How does Robert Fulghum's behavior change after he learns the significance of the items in the bag?

Why does Robert Fulghum treasure the bag?

▼ Discuss

If you were to put together a bag of items you treasure, what would go into it? Why?

In your own words, what does the phrase, "standing knee-deep in the river and dying of thirst" mean?

What message do you get from "The Good Stuff"?

▼ Write

Recognize Tone Tone is an author's attitude toward the subject. It is his or her manner of speaking, and it reveals the writer's emotional attitude. Quickly write down how Robert Fulghum feels about himself, about his and Molly's actions, and about the contents of the bag. Discuss with a partner what Fulghum's tone in "The Good Stuff" is and how the tone is different in different parts of the essay.

Write an Essay Have you ever received a memorable present? Write a short essay describing the gift, when you received it, and your feelings about it then and now. What tone will you use to add depth and feeling to your essay?

Los Ancianos[1]

Pat Mora

They hold hands
as they walk with slow steps.
Careful together they cross the plaza
both slightly stooped, bodies returning to the land,
he in faded khaki and straw hat,
she wrapped in soft clothes, black
rebozo[2] round her head and shoulders.

Tourists in halter tops and shorts
pose by flame trees and fountains,
but the old couple walks step by step
on the edge.
Even in the heat, only their wrinkled
hands and faces show.   They know
of moving through a crowd at their own pace.

I watch him help her
off the curb and I smell love
like dried flowers, old love
of holding hands with one man for fifty years.

Can you tell what people are like just by watching them? Picture the scene as you read this poem.

[1] *Spanish:* old ones
[2] *Spanish:* shawl

Responding to the Poem

▼ Think Back

How does the speaker know that the old couple are in love?

How does the couple differ from the people around them?

▼ Discuss

Do you think you could be in love with the same man or woman for fifty years? Why or why not?

Why would the poet write a poem about a seemingly ordinary couple?

▼ Write

Write Similes In "Los Ancianos," the speaker states that she can "smell love/like dried flowers." This description is a *simile*, a comparison of two unlike things that includes *like, than,* or *as.* Create a list of similes to describe an elderly couple in love.

About the Author

Pat Mora was born in El Paso, Texas, in 1942, and now lives in Ohio. Best known for her poems, she also writes stories and articles for periodicals. One reason she writes is to present a Hispanic perspective as part of our literary heritage. She also writes "because I am fascinated by the pleasure and power of words."

Mark Messner

Mitch Albom

I sn't life funny, Mark Messner thought. He held a spoonful of malted shake up to his father's lips, which were black and peeling, burned from chemotherapy.[1] "Here you go, Dad," he said. His father rolled his eyes and made a "mmm" sound, like a child. Mark smiled, pulled the spoon out and dug it back into the cup.

Isn't life funny? A few weeks ago, Messner, 22, was a rookie linebacker for the Los Angeles Rams. He was getting paid to play football. He was living in sunny southern California. Then the phone rang. "You'd better come home," his sister said. He knew what that meant. He left the team, without pay, and boarded a plane for Detroit.

When he first saw his father, lying in the hospital bed, Mark bit his lip. Then he went out in the hall and began to sob. He showed the nurse an old photo, before the disease, and she said, "Oh, my God."

Although this true story won an award for Best Feature Story for Sports in 1990, it's not about a great pass or a touchdown. It is about a football player who is a champion off as well as on the field.

[1] the use of chemicals to treat cancer

Now he sat by the bed and fed his father, the way Del Pretty had done for him when he was an infant. Of course, technically, Del was his stepfather, but Mark never cared for that phrase. He figured if the man raised me, fed me, spanked me, hugged me, took me to school, wrote me poems, came to all my football games and made me feel like the most important person in the world, well, the hell with it. He is my father.

And I am his son.

"Have some more, Dad," he whispered. He looked at the blotches of red along Del's arms and legs. He saw the blood stains on the sheets where the skin had peeled away. He thought back to a year ago, when life seemed so carefree. He was heading to the Rose Bowl with the Michigan Wolverines. There would be Hawaii after that and Japan after that. And then came the NFL draft. The Rams took him with a low-round pick. Then in training camp they had him carrying the red cones up and down the field, like some equipment boy.

"Dad," Mark said one night in a phone call home. "You'd better pull my resume[2] off my computer. I can't compete on this level."

"Just keep plugging," Del said.

"But they got me *moving cones!*"

"They didn't draft you to move cones."

What does he know? Mark thought. He's never been in the NFL. He owns a piano store, for Pete's sake. But eventually the Rams did come around. He stopped moving cones. He played in the exhibition games. He made the team. His father had been right. Again.

[2] a summary of a person's education and employment, used when applying for jobs

Mark looked at him. The room was quiet. He dug the spoon into the melting chocolate.

Take the chemo, they had told him.

"No," he had said.

"There's no alternative."

"There's got to be an alternative."

Del Pretty had been diagnosed as having lymph node cancer in 1980. He fought the very idea, as if it had somehow insulted his pride. He scorned[3] chemotherapy, because he felt it would deteriorate[4] him. Instead he searched for other methods. He tried special diets and experimental drugs. And eventually he beat the illness into remission.[5] Who had time to be sick? There was the business. The family. And Mark's football games.

"He never missed one," Mark recalls. "He came to all the home games at Michigan and a lot of the road ones, too. There was this game in Indiana where the weather was horrible. He sat there in the rain the whole time."

Not that he was one of those jock-hungry fathers. On the contrary, Del Pretty was *not* a very athletic man. Silver-haired, dapper,[6] with glasses and a gentle but disciplined expression, he looked more like a well-placed accountant. Which he was. But he loved his children. He would show his feelings quietly, in notes that Mark found in his college mailbox: *"Dear Mark, I want you to know how proud you make me feel."*

Mark's friends would tease him sometimes about how close he was with Del. It was almost corny.

[3] rejected as wrong

[4] to become worse

[5] the lessening or disappearance of symptoms of a disease

[6] smartly dressed

He had chosen Michigan over UCLA because he wanted Del to be able to see him play. Before he left for the Rams, Mark gave his Dad a record. "Wind Beneath My Wings" by Bette Midler. He told him to listen to the words, because that's how he felt. *"Did I ever tell you you're my hero. You're everything I wish I could be."*

It was the stuff of sappy movies. Unless you know the whole story. Mark was the son of divorce. Several times, his mother married and remarried. His natural father (Max Messner, a former NFL player) also remarried. The one constant in his life was Del. He was there when Mark had problems. He was there when Mark wanted to talk about life, or girls, or football. He gave honest answers. Strict, but from the heart.

When Del and Mark's mother divorced, it tore Mark apart. His Dad had to live alone in some apartment in Northville. Why? It's not fair.

And then the cancer came back.

Take the chemo, they told him.

"No," he said.

Once again he tried experimental drugs. He flew to Houston for a new pill. He flew to California for a procedure in which animals are injected with samples from the patient's tumors, then the antibodies formed are injected into the patient.

"I'm sorry," the doctor said. "The process takes six to eight months."

"Yes?" said Del.

"Well, quite frankly, I don't think you have that long."

What do you do when a doctor tells you that? Already the disease had changed him physically. The tumors were stealing nutrients from his food and releasing lymph fluid instead into his abdomen. He was bloated like a pregnant woman.

"He couldn't sleep in a bed anymore," says Messner. "His stomach was so large. But meanwhile, the rest of his body was suffering from malnutrition."[7]

[7] a condition of poor nourishment due to illness or improper diet

Alone, out of options, he went to doctors in Ann Arbor. "Chemotherapy," they said. It was early fall. Football season. Mark was in L.A., getting paid. It was as if Del had held out all this time, just to make sure his son could handle adulthood.

"All right," Del said, finally. "I'll try the chemotherapy."

They put the needle in his arm.

The blotches began after the second treatment. They looked like a rash. He asked his doctor. "Must be a skin condition," they said. "Have you changed your soap recently?"

His soap?

Another round of chemo, an increased dosage. Now the skin began to pus and fester. Like a horrible sunburn, it would die and peel away. His back. His legs. Around his mouth. Without so much as a match's flame, he was burnt all over.

"It was the chemo," says Mark now. "And what was happening outside was happening inside him as well. The organs were being destroyed." How could this be? Wasn't chemo supposed to help him? You would touch his back and the skin would come off in your hands. One time, a nurse tried rubbing ointment on the sores. Del began to moan in pain. Mark came running in.

"What's wrong, what's he saying?" the nurse asked.

"He's saying don't rub, don't rub," said Mark. "It hurts too much."

This was the horrible reality: Del Pretty was dying, one layer at a time. Few of us could witness such a thing.

But the love between son and father is like God's muscle. So while his teammates worked out back in Los Angeles, Mark Messner came to Harper Grace hospital every morning, 10 A.M., two hours before visiting time, to bathe his father.

He would lift him with his powerful arms and slide him gently into the tub. Sheets of bloody skin would stick to his hands, get under his fingernails. He did not flinch. He poured cool water over his father's body and comforted him. While Del could still speak, Mark held the phone to his ear and let him talk to the office at Hammell Music, the piano store which he owned in Livonia. Together they went over the books of the church where Del was treasurer.

When Del's vocal cords no longer worked, Mark did the talking. When Del's eyesight went, Mark would tell him what he was missing.

On November 25, they put the Michigan–Ohio State game on TV. Del stayed awake for the entire thing. When the final gun sounded, Mark said "Hey, Dad! How about that? They're going to the Rose Bowl!"

Del raised his arm and made a soft fist. He shook it once.

Two days later, he died.

Mark knew as soon as the phone rang. It was 4 A.M. His mother was crying in the other room. "Mom," he whispered, "they said Dad expired."[8]

He paused.

"It makes him sound like a license plate."

At the funeral, Mark read a poem Del had sent him this fall. And when they closed the casket, Mark's Rose Bowl watch was around his father's wrist. Before it was always Del taking care of business matters, but now Mark handled the arrangements. He signed the papers. He went through the bills. He re-read the old letters and thought about their final moments together in the hospital, the feeding, the bathing. The circle was complete. The child had become father to the man.

"You know," Messner says now. "I was never embarrassed in the hospital. All that blood and skin, that was just his body. It was his heart that I was dealing with. I would have done anything for him. Anything."

Today, Mark will play a football game for the Rams, the regular season finale.

[8] died

When it is over he will go to call his father, as he always did. And instead, he will have to close his eyes and imagine. "I know he's watching," he says without sadness. "He used to joke about having a beer with God. I'll bet he's doing it now."

You hear about the decline of the American family, how the old are tossed aside by the young. And then you hear of a kid who left pro football to tend to his dying father. These are the last words of the poem Del wrote, which Mark read at his funeral:

"If all else in a man's life added to zero, no greater success than to be counted his son's hero."

Isn't life funny? It takes us and leaves us. And love endures. Monday is Christmas, and that means this: Count your blessings, everybody, count them all very carefully. One precious person at a time.

About the Author

Mitch Albom was born in Passaic, New Jersey, in 1958. He has been a reporter and a cohost of a sports talk show. He currently writes a sports column for the *Detroit Free Press*. He has earned national attention and awards for his columns, which highlight examples of athletic courage and determination. In addition to newspaper writing, Albom authored *Fab Five*, a book about a legendary basketball team. He also co-authored *Bo*, the biography of Bo Schembechler, a well-known former University of Michigan football coach.

Responding to the Story

▼ Think Back

What was Mark Messner's family life like?

In what ways did Del Pretty influence Mark Messner?

How does Mark Messner become "father to the man" in his relationship with Del Pretty?

▼ Discuss

Are the roles between parents and children sometimes reversed? Explain.

Del Pretty wrote, "If all else in a man's life added to zero, no greater success than to be counted his son's hero." Do you agree with this? Why or why not?

▼ Write

Describe the Tone How does Mitch Albom feel about Mark, Del, and Del's fight with cancer? The words a writer uses and the descriptions of characters and events all can reveal the tone—the author's attitude towards the subject. Describe Albom's tone, using details from the essay to support your opinion.

Write an Essay Have you ever been deeply affected by either a tragic or an uplifting event? How are your feelings now different than they were then? Write a short essay describing the situation. What tone will you use to help readers understand your feelings?

Mother

Bea Exner Liu

I wish that I could talk with her again.

That's what I thought of when I thought of home,

Always supposing I had a home to come to.

If she were here, we'd warm the Chinese pot

To brew a jasmine-scented elixir,[1]

And I would tell her how my life has been—

All the parts that don't make sense to me—

And she would let me talk until the parts

Fitted together.

That will never be.

She couldn't wait for me to come to her—

Ten years away. I couldn't wish for her

To wait, all blind and helpless as she was.

So now I have come home to emptiness:

When a mother dies before her daughter can see her one more time, what does the daughter wish for?

[1] cure-all

No silly welcome-rhyme, no happy tears,

No eager questioning. No way to get

An answer to my questions. Silence fills

The rooms that once were cheery with her song,

And all the things I wanted to talk out

With her are locked forever in my heart.

I wander through the rooms where she is not.

Alone I sit on the hassock[2] by her chair,   [2] a cushioned footstool

And there, at last, I seem to hear her voice:

"You're a big girl now. You can work things out."

About the Author

**Bea Exner Liu won an award for her children's book,
Little Wu and the Watermelons, which is about a boy
living in China during the war with Japan. In the story,
Ms. Liu explores the relationship between the boy and
his mother. She is also the author of a recently published
memoir, *Remembering China, 1935–1945*.**

Responding to the Poem

▼ Think Back

What does the daughter think of as she walks through her mother's house?

What does the daughter miss most about her mother?

How does the tone, or feeling, of the poem change in the last line?

▼ Discuss

In the last two lines, the daughter imagines her mother talking to her. Does the daughter feel comforted by these imagined words, or do they upset her? Explain.

What is the key feeling you get from this poem? What message can be learned from it?

▼ Write

Identify Main Ideas The poem is divided into three units, or stanzas. Each stanza develops a new thought in much the same way that a paragraph does in prose writing. Quickly write the main idea of each stanza. How does the poet make the transition from stanza to stanza?

Write a Poem Write a poem in which you describe the things that you look forward to whenever you enter some special or familiar place—your home, a friend's house, or a favorite store or restaurant. Use stanzas to organize your poem. Try to include images that appeal to the senses.

The Night We Started Dancing

Ann Cameron

I am named after my dad, Luis, but everybody calls me Luisito. I live with my grandfather and grandmother; my four uncles; my two aunts; my cousin, Diego; a girl named Maria who helps my grandmother; our two dogs, Chubby and Pilot; our two cats, Stripes and Hunter; and our big green parrot, Bright Star, that my grandmother always says she is going to bake and serve for dinner someday.

We live in a town called Santa Cruz, in Guatemala, Central America. Santa Cruz has a park where there are great band concerts, free, every week. It has a public school, and a big college for army cadets, and it has an electronics store where you could special-order a computer, but it doesn't have paved streets, it has only dirt streets that turn to dust in the winter when it's dry, and to mud in the summer when it rains.

I like dirt streets. It goes with the special thing about Santa Cruz, which is that it's a very old town. It was a town before Columbus discovered America, and

Families are shaped by the experiences they share. What event has overshadowed the lives of Luisito and his family?

before the Spaniards came from Spain to steal our land and our gold and make slaves of people, because they said their religion was the true one, and God liked them better than us.

On the edge of Santa Cruz there is a high hill covered with old pine trees and the ruins of pyramids[1] and an ancient fortress. That's where the headquarters of our people was, the headquarters of the kingdom of the Quichés, where our ancestors[2] fought the Spaniards harder than anybody in Guatemala, before they lost for good.

Once, when I was six, a real Spaniard from Spain came to our house for dinner. He was going to do some business with my grandfather, so my grandmother invited him.

The whole dinner I kept watching my grandfather and the Spaniard all the time, and looking at my grandfather's big machete knife that he keeps by the front door.

Finally, I couldn't stand it. "*Con permiso*, excuse me," and got up from the table and followed my grandmother into the kitchen when she went to get more food, and I even ducked under Bright Star's perch to get there faster.

"When?" I asked my grandmother. "When is he going to do it?"

"Who?" my grandmother said. "Do what?"

"When is Grandpa going to kill the Spaniard?" I whispered, and Bright Star hissed in his loudest voice, "Kill the Spaniard!" and the Spaniard looked around fast and dropped his fork.

[1] large structures, each with a square base and four sloping triangular sides meeting at the top

[2] people from whom one is descended; forefathers

My grandfather stopped munching his tortilla. "Don't be concerned," he said to the Spaniard, "we just have a crazy parrot," and my grandmother said, "One day I am going to bake you, Bright Star!"

"Are you crazy?" my grandmother said. "How can the Spaniard help being a Spaniard? He was born one, just like you were born a Guatemalan and a Quiché."

Then she took me into one of the bedrooms and closed the door.

"What is this all about?" she said. "Why would Grandpa kill the Spaniard?"

"For being a Spaniard, " I said.

"Are you crazy?" my grandmother said. "How can the Spaniard help being a Spaniard? He was born one, just like you were born a Guatemalan and a Quiché. Don't you know the battles with the Spaniards were over hundreds of years ago? We have to judge people by what they do, not by where they come from. And we have to fight our own battles, too, not the ones our ancestors fought."

So that was when I first found out that we'd never get our kingdom back—at least not the way it used to be.

My grandfather was born poor, and he never went to school. He worked from the time he was six years old, out in the wheat fields and the cornfields, hoeing. Every day when he finished work and went home, he would pass by his own dad in the street, drinking and spending all the family money. My great-granddad never helped my granddad at all. But my granddad just kept working, and when he was twenty, he started buying land—pieces nobody thought were good for anything—and on the land he planted apple orchards, and when the apples grew all over, big and beautiful, he got rich. He built a big house for my grandmother and our family, with five big bedrooms, and a patio in the middle full of flowers, and a living room where he and my grandmother put up all the pictures of both their families, except my grandfather never put up a picture of his dad. Then, last year, he must have finally started feeling sorry for his father, because he got his picture out of a drawer, and dusted it off, and put it up in the living room, only not with the rest of the pictures. So now my great-grandfather is staring out at the rest of the family, kind of ashamed-looking, from behind a fern.

My grandmother only learned to read four years ago, but she made my aunts and uncles study hard in school, and now she's making me do it, too. When I asked her why I had to study so hard, she said, "So that you aren't working with a hoe in the fields all your life, with the sun beating down on your head like a hammer."

When my grandparents' kids got to be old enough to study in the capital, my grandparents bought a house there for them to live in. So most of the year my aunts and uncles are there, studying architecture, and economics, and dentistry, and law, and accounting, and psychology. Only my youngest aunt, Celia, who is sixteen, is still living in Santa Cruz all the time. But next year she's going to the capital, too. She says she's going to study to be a doctor. My grandparents are very proud of all their children. The sad thing is, their oldest son, the only one who was studying agriculture and who loved the land the way my grandfather does, was my father, and he died. My mother died with him.

My mother was teaching grade school and my dad was in the last year of his agriculture studies when they died. I was four years old.

It happened four years ago, when my mom and dad and I and Uncle Ricardo were taking a bus from the capital to go back to my grandparents' house for Christmas. The bus terminal was full of dust and people trying to sell ice cream and coconuts and last-minute Christmas presents. Lots of people were going back to their hometowns for the holidays, and there weren't enough buses. Everybody was pushing and shoving to get on the ones there were.

My mom had a suitcase, and my dad had me on his back because he figured I couldn't run fast enough, and Uncle Ricardo was staring toward the sun with his hand shading his eyes, trying to see the bus that goes to Santa Cruz.

"Santa Cruz! That's it! Run!" he shouted, and my mom and dad raced for the front door of the bus, and Uncle Ricardo raced for the back, and they did flying dives over the top of a bunch of other people. My mom and dad got seats right behind the driver, and I sat on my mom's lap. Uncle Ricardo got stuck at the back, standing up.

Everybody pushed the windows down to get more air, and the driver put the bus in gear, but it didn't move, and his helper, the ticket taker, got out a hammer and a wrench and raised the hood on the bus and hammered on something for a while, and then the driver tried to move the bus again, and it went, and Uncle Ricardo heard my mother say, "A miracle! What a miraculous miracle!" and the ticket taker ran after the moving bus and jumped in the open door with the hammer and the wrench in his hand, and we were off.

Uncle Ricardo settled in and tried to take his elbow out of the stomach of the person on his right, and get his feet out from under the feet of the person on his left. My mom and dad were probably about the only ones who could see out the window, and who knew how the driver was driving.

The bus didn't go very fast, because it couldn't with so many people on it, but after a while Uncle Ricardo felt the bus lurch, and he heard my dad say to the driver, "Be careful, brother!" so he figured that the bus driver must have been taking a chance passing on a mountain curve.

A little while later he felt the bus twist again, and he heard my father say to the driver, "A man who foresees trouble and prevents it, is worth two men." But it seemed like the driver didn't feel like listening, because a little while later Uncle Ricardo heard my father say, "No matter where you are going, you don't have to get there first. The thing is, to get there."

And after that he heard my mother say, "Driver, there is more time than life."

And that was all he heard, except for my mother's voice just once more, shouting, "Luisito!" just before my father grabbed me with one hand and threw me out the window.

The bus driver went head-on into another bus. And my mother was right, because time just keeps going on and on and on, but she and my dad and the bus driver and the ticket taker and a lot of other people ran out of life completely.

Uncle Ricardo was okay because he was at the back, and I was okay.

The only part I remember begins with the grip of my father's hand, and how it hurt when he shoved me through the window frame. But I don't like to remember. I like to think about daytime things, my aunts and uncles, and things that are happening now.

But sometimes I still dream about it, being thrown out the window. In the dream I am little again, the same age I was then, and I land down a hillside in a freshly hoed field, just the way I really landed, but it is not daytime, it is almost completely dark, and I get up and go back to the wrecked bus, to find my mom and dad, but it gets darker and darker, and I never can find them.

Uncle Ricardo says one day I won't have the dream anymore. He says that my parents loved me a lot, and that I will always have them in my heart. He says one day my dream self will understand that, too. It will know that my parents are always with me when I remember them. It won't have to go back to the wrecked bus to look for them anymore.

And really I am okay, and Uncle Ricardo is okay, and my grandmother also is okay, because she loves all her children very much, but equally. The only one who has not been okay is my grandfather, because he loved my dad more than anybody. My dad wasn't only his son, he was his best friend.

The first Christmas after the accident we didn't celebrate, because nobody wanted to. But the next Christmas we didn't celebrate either, because Grandpa didn't want to. On the anniversary of the accident, he cut a lot of white roses and put them in front of my parents' wedding picture that hangs in the living room, and we visited their graves at the cemetery, so that was all there was of Christmas that year, too.

And from the beginning my grandmother said we shouldn't mention my mom and dad in front of my grandfather because it might upset him too much. She said we should just wait, and in time he would get better.

But it got to be September of the third year after my father died, and my grandfather still wasn't any better. My aunt Patricia, who had been leaving my cousin Diego with us a lot in Santa Cruz, decided to take Diego to the city. She said it was because she didn't have so many courses and she would have more time to spend with him, but Uncle Ricardo told me it was really because she thought it was too gloomy for Diego around our house.

She wanted to develop four new laughs, even though my grandmother said it was a waste of time, and she couldn't see what was wrong with the laugh Celia was born with.

The only reason I liked being in the house is that I like my grandmother and Celia a lot, my grandmother because she never yells at anybody, and Celia because she treats me like a grown-up. She got me to help her with a lot of projects, especially her Laugh Development Project, in which she said she needed the opinion of a man.

She wanted to develop four new laughs, even though my grandmother said it was a waste of time, and she couldn't see what was wrong with the laugh Celia was born with.

Celia said these are modern times, and a person should have five of everything. She said her original laugh was for when she really felt like laughing, and the other four would be for when she couldn't afford to be serious. She wanted my opinion because she wanted to make sure the four new laughs would be good enough to impress boyfriends.

So when Grandpa wasn't around, she practiced in front of the big cracked mirror on the patio.

"Hah, hah, HAH, HAH, hah," went the first laugh, which is a rapid one where she tosses her long black hair back behind her shoulders. That is her Rio de Janeiro laugh.

"Ho ho ho," she laughs slowly, and rubs her chin thoughtfully with the finger of one hand. That's her Paris laugh.

"Hee hee hee," she giggles, and covers her eyes with her hands. That's her Tahiti laugh.

"Hoo, hoo, hoo, hoo," she laughs, and raises her eyebrows very high. That's her Mexico City laugh.

She got all the ideas for the laughs from TV and from fashion magazines. After she got them all worked out, I told her they were all good, except the Tahiti laugh, which looked like she was just waking up in the morning, so she decided to rename it a waking-up laugh, to throw a stretch into it.

So she did. But just when she had them all perfect, Bright Star got them perfect, too. He sang them all off in a row, and then he said, in my voice, "Laugh Development Project."

"Now I can't bring any boyfriend home!" Celia said. "Either I can't bring one home, or I can't use my laughs."

"Not only that," I said, "Grandpa is going to know about this for sure."

Celia shrugged. "Maybe he'll borrow a laugh," she said. "He doesn't seem to have one of his own. Anyway, what more can he do? We already don't have Christmas anymore."

Sure enough, when Grandpa came home, Bright Star talked. He laughed all four laughs, and then imitated me, saying "Laugh Development Project."

It happened at dinner. My grandfather looked at Bright Star, and he looked at Celia, and he looked at me, but all he said was, "After school tomorrow, I want to take you out to the orchards, Luisito."

So I said okay, and the next afternoon we hiked out to the orchards.

"You are around your Aunt Celia too much," my grandfather said, but not unkindly. "You need the influence of a man."

"I am a man," I said.

"You are?" my grandfather said. "How do you know?"

"Celia said so."

He looked at me and said it took more than Celia's saying so to make somebody a man, and then he started telling me about the trees, and what you had to do to take care of them, and how many different kinds of apples there were, and how you could tell them apart.

But a bad thing happened, because the orchards are right next to the pyramids and the forts of the old kingdom, and I kept thinking about them and wanting to go over there, instead of listening to my grandfather.

"Luisito," he said suddenly, "How many kinds of apples do I have?"

And I couldn't tell him.

"You're not listening! Your father understood and remembered everything when he was your age!" he shouted. "Go on home to your grandmother!"

So I left, and instead of going straight home, I went over to the pyramids and ran up to the top of the biggest and stood there listening to the branches of the pine trees in the wind. It didn't help anything. And then I walked home alone.

When I told my grandma what happened, she said, "Your dad did understand and remember very well when he was your age. But when he was your age, he also played with matches once and set a whole cornfield on fire. It took us, the neighbors and the whole fire department to put it out."

"Tell Grandpa that!" I said. "Remind him about it!"

"I will sometime," my grandmother said, "but not now."

"When?" I asked. "You said Grandpa would get better and we just had to be patient. He used to make jokes, Celia says. He used to take everybody on trips. Now he never does, and he never gets any better."

"You are right," my grandmother said.

"Besides," I said, "Christmas is coming, and I am tired of not having Christmas, and so is Celia."

"You're probably right," my grandmother said. "We should celebrate Christmas."

And she actually used the telephone, which she never uses, to call up Ricardo and talk to him about it.

And that night at dinner, she told my grandfather, "It's time we started to celebrate Christmas again."

"I would rather not," my grandfather said.

"The children say they won't come home for Christmas, unless we celebrate, like the old days. Luis and Celia say they would rather go into the city to be with Ricardo and everybody if we don't celebrate Christmas."

"Um," my grandfather said.

"I might go, too," my grandmother said.

"*You* might go?" my grandfather said.

"Yes, I probably will go," my grandmother said.

"You would *leave* me?" my grandfather said.

"Just for Christmas," my grandmother said.

"It wouldn't be good," my grandfather said. "We've been together thirty-one years. You've never been away. Not one day!"

"Times change," my grandmother said.

"Well," my grandfather said, "we had better celebrate Christmas. But I won't dance."

"You don't have to dance," my grandmother said. "Nobody has to dance. But at least we will have dance music, anyway."

Celia and I made a beautiful golden Christmas tree out of corn husks that we cut to fasten on wires and make the shape of branches. When we were done, the tree went all the way to the ceiling, and we draped it with red chains of tinsel. And my grandmother stood in front of the stove all Christmas Eve day making the tamales for the midnight dinner—corn stuffed with chicken and meat and olives and raisins and hot chili sauce, and wrapped in banana leaves to cook. And everybody arrived from the city about six-thirty at night, just in time for the supper we were going to have to tide us over to the real dinner at midnight.

Uncle Ricardo brought Diego and me about sixty firecrackers to set off at midnight, when all the kids in town go outside to set off firecrackers, so we were feeling good. And my grandfather had dressed up in his best and happiest clothes, new pants, and a cap that makes him look as young as my uncles.

Everybody hugged, and we all sat down to eat, but nobody talked much until we were almost finished, when Aunt Patricia said, "All the same, it's sad anyway."

And my Uncle Pedro, who had been an exchange student in the U.S. for one year of high school, said, "If the roads had shoulders, the way the highways do in the U.S., they never would have died."

And Celia said, "So in the great U.S.A. there are no traffic accidents?"

And before Pedro could answer her, my grandfather got up out of his chair and went out on the patio, and we all stopped talking.

"Luisito," my grandmother said, "go be with your grandfather."

So I went out on the patio and stood by my grandfather, who was looking up at the sky and wouldn't look down.

I just stood there by him, looking up, too.

There was a full moon, shining down on the patio and on the papery violet leaves of the bougainvillea, and my grandfather spoke, in a choked voice.

"See the leaves? There are so many you can't see the branch, and all different.

"And we are like them, all different, but holding on to an invisible branch—but two of us are missing!

"Why do they have to talk about it? Don't they know I've cried enough? What do they think I do out in the orchard, but cry?"

"You should cry with us," I said, and I saw my grandfather's eyes drop tears, and we stood there a long time.

Everybody else had gone into the living room, and while we were standing there, the dance music started, very slowly, low music, soft like smoke, winding into the moonlight.

"Oh, Luisito," my grandfather said. "What can we do? What can anybody do? Luisito, we should dance."

And so my granddad and I danced, around the cage of Bright Star, who was sleeping under a new Christmas blanket, and past the cracked mirror and the bougainvillaea vine, and then, very slowly, into the living room. And then I danced with Celia, and my grandfather put his arms around my grandmother and danced with her, and everybody danced with everybody, straight through until midnight when the fireworks started going off in huge booms all over town, and we all held hands, and everyone of us kissed every other one, and I noticed for the first time in a long time that in the photo of my mom and dad, above Grandpa's white roses, they were smiling.

About the Author

Ann Cameron was born in 1943 in Rice Lake, Wisconsin. She is the author of numerous children's books, including *The Stories Julian Tells* and *The Most Beautiful Place in the World*, a Jane Addams Children's Award Honor Book. Cameron lives in Guatemala, where she has served as the volunteer director of the municipal library. Her latest book, *The Kidnapped Prince*, is based on the true story of an African boy who was kidnapped and later freed.

Responding to the Story

▼ Think Back

How does Luisito feel about his ancestors and his cultural heritage? What details give you clues?

Why doesn't Luisito's grandfather respect his own father?

Why does the grandfather finally decide to celebrate Christmas? Why does he dance?

▼ Discuss

Luisito's grandmother says, "We have to judge people by what they do, not by where they come from. And we have to fight our own battles, too, not the ones our ancestors fought." Is this good advice? Can you think of situations today to which this advice could be applied?

What do you think Luisito's grandfather learns on Christmas night?

▼ Write

Write a Flashback Ann Cameron describes how Luisito's parents died in a flashback, which is an interruption of a story's narrative in order to present an earlier scene or episode. Is there another part of the story that would make an interesting flashback? Write a short flashback of that scene.

Write Another Flashback Think about stories you've read. Is there one that seems to be missing information? Write a flashback to clarify any confusing parts.

Theme Links

Expressions of Love

In this unit, you've read selections about romantic love as well as about love of family. You have also thought about your own feelings of love and how you express them.

▼ Group Discussion

With a partner or in a small group, talk about the selections in this unit and how they relate to the theme and to your own lives. Use questions like the following to guide the discussion.

- What different kinds of love are there?
- How do you express different kinds of love?
- In what similar ways do people throughout the world express their love for others?
- Did any of the characters in these selections fail to express their love? How?

▼ Meet the Characters

Work in small groups. Imagine that each of you is a character or person from one of the selections in the unit. Take turns giving and receiving advice on how to effectively express your love for others. Invite members of the class to comment on the advice.

▼ Songs of Love

Songwriters have been expressing their feelings for years by writing songs of love. Many are about romantic love. Others are about love for family members or friends. What are your favorite songs of love? With a partner or in a small group, gather audio copies of these songs. Have a classroom concert. Play each song and discuss who the narrator of the song is and who is the beloved. Also discuss what everyone likes or dislikes about each song.

Write your own songs of love. Take turns singing the songs as classmates record them onto a tape.

▼ The Theme and You

Many people find it difficult to tell another person that they love him or her. Write a brief note to another person—father, mother, sibling, close friend—in which you tell the person why you love him or her and what your relationship means to you. You do not have to share the note with the person.

Special
People

Some people, such as musicians or athletes, are special because they have a talent or skill. Great leaders, scientists, and astronauts are special because of their roles in history. Ordinary people can be special too. Someone who overcomes a handicap or works with poor people or runs a community's Fourth of July parade is special. Someone who is an important part of your life, like a close relative, might be very special to you.

Make a list of people that you think are "special." Who is on your list? You can probably think of many different ways in which someone is special enough to be included.

As you read these selections, think about why the writers thought the people they wrote about were special. Then think about the people on your list. What makes each of them special? What did they do?

Grandma Traub

Amy Ling

Everything about her said, "Surplus":[1]
extra chins, flaps of loose flesh,
flocks of freckles,

In these poems, Amy
Ling writes about two
special grandmothers.
What words does Ling
use to help you picture
how different the two
women are?

here and there a wart;
her dresses yards of georgette[2]
set off with brooches,
twisted strands of pearls;
her white hair, sometimes dyed blue
to keep the yellow out, rolled up
round her head like a halo.

Love too she had in surplus,
left her own Pennsylvania Dutch
to sail clear to China
brought the Bible and modern medicine,
became head nurse,
director of Yoyang hospital,
adopted my mother when her mother died.

[1] extra; excess

[2] a thin, crinkled fabric

Retired and back home,
in sensible low heels
black and laced up high,
behind round wire-rimmed glasses
her blue eyes delighted in us,
her Chinese grandchildren.
She tucked us into her home,
cooked shoo fly pie, fresh donuts,
dandelion salads, tapioca puddings;
read Bambi, Heidi, Pollyanna,
transformed leftover cloth
into flowers for our quilts.

For Christmas and birthdays,
she was giving me one at a time
a wedding party of dolls:
the tall bride in proud white satin,
bridesmaids in rose and powder blue.
She was just making a suit
for the undersized groom,
this large woman who never married,
when she died.

Grandma Ling

A m y   L i n g

If you dig that hole deep enough,
you'll reach China, they used to tell me,
a child in a backyard in Pennsylvania.
Not strong enough to dig that hole,
I waited twenty years,
then sailed back, half way around the world.

In Taiwan I first met Grandma.
Before she came to view, I heard
her slippered feet softly measure
the tatami[3] floor with even step;
the aqua paper-covered door slid open
and there I faced
my five foot height, sturdy legs and feet,
square forehead, high cheeks and wide-set eyes;
my image stood before me,
acted on by fifty years.

[3] a floor mat made of straw

She smiled, stretched her arms
to take to heart the eldest daughter
of her youngest son a quarter century away.
She spoke a tongue I knew no word of,
and I was sad I could not understand,
but I could hug her.

About the Author

Amy Ling was born in 1939 in Beijing, China, and came to the United States at the age of six. Ling is a teacher as well as a poet, an editor, and an author of TV scripts, stories, and articles. She has served as Director of the Asian American Studies Program at the University of Wisconsin. Ling is the author of *Between Worlds: Women Writers of Chinese Ancestry*, *Chinamerican Reflections*, and numerous articles and reviews. The poems "Grandma Ling" and "Grandma Traub" are autobiographical.

Responding to the Poems

▼ Think Back

Describe Grandma Ling and Grandma Traub.

How did Grandma Traub become Amy Ling's grandma?

According to Amy Ling, what were Grandma Traub's most endearing qualities?

▼ Discuss

Amy Ling says that she could not understand Grandma Ling's language. How might they communicate?

What kind of poems are these? What do you think Amy Ling hoped to accomplish by writing about Grandma Ling and Grandma Traub?

▼ Write

Analyze Imagery Amy Ling tries to recapture how her Grandma Traub looked and the qualities that made her special. She creates vivid images made up of sensory details. Skim the selection to find memorable images. List those images. Write a summary of why they are effective.

Write a Poem Write a poem in which you describe meeting a relative for the first time. Use vivid images and descriptive details to communicate your feelings before, during, and after the meeting. Break your poem into stanzas to help develop and connect ideas.

The Education of a Woman Golfer

Nancy Lopez

The real indication that I might indeed turn out to be the golfer my parents hoped I'd be came within a year after my first experience on Roswell's municipal[1] course. I was entered in a PeeWee tournament being held in Alamogordo, New Mexico, for girls between the ages of eight and twelve. It was a twenty-seven-hole affair held over a three-day period and I won it by a margin of 110 strokes! Dad was so excited and pleased that as an extra prize he bought me my favorite present at that time, a Barbie doll! That set a dangerously expensive precedent[2] for him, because I was so crazy about Barbie dolls that I never could get too many. It wasn't that I actually played with them the way I did when I was even younger, but I had begun to be a collector. You've heard of the fastest gun in the West? Well I was building up the biggest collection of Barbie dolls in the West. Each time after that when I did something special in golf, Dad came through with a doll that meant more to me than any medal or cup. By

Nancy Lopez was one of America's top professional women golfers. Who does she thank for her success?

[1] public; belonging to a city or town

[2] a standard to serve as a guide in the future

the time I was twelve I already had a great many and then, when I won the Women's State Amateur (Women's, not Girls') at that age, he came home with a whole armful! I may have reached the ripe old age of twelve, and I may have shot a course record of 75 at the University South course in Albuquerque in the run toward winning the state championship, but collecting Barbie dolls was still Big Stuff! Dad said, "Nancy win. Nancy get every doll in the shop!"

You may have noticed the way Dad speaks? We are, of course, Mexican Americans, and that brings up another obstacle to my getting an easy early golf education. Dad has a strong Spanish accent and flavor to his speech and, although that didn't rub off on a girl who grew up so Americanized as I did in school and with Anglo friends, all of us Lopezes are definitely and unashamedly Mexican Americans in Roswell, a town where that surely wasn't a social asset.[3] It's a very pleasant town of some 40,000 people, and I have good memories of it, but we had the sort of minority status that minorities invariably suffer everywhere. In my case, it certainly never was any tragedy, and just about all of my friends were Anglos and good friends, but one could get snubbed when one least expected it. I remember once dating a boy and his parents hit the roof when they heard about it. Today when someone tells me that certain old "friends" from Roswell send me warm regards, I sometimes have to take it with a grain of salt. A few of those old "friends" don't raise tender memories.

[3] a useful or desirable thing

The point is that while I could play on the municipal course, that wasn't a well-kept, regulation layout that could have challenged my developing game better. It was only a nine-hole layout then, not well trapped, and its chief virtue was that you could play there for something like $1.25. Roswell had several things to boast about, including being John Denver's hometown, but one of its prides was the country club with its first-rate golf course. The dues there would have been pretty tough for Dad to manage, but the whole idea was academic[4] anyhow. Mexican Americans like my parents would not have been welcome members, and if they didn't join I obviously couldn't and wouldn't. As a matter of fact, I'm sure I wouldn't have been happy in that atmosphere[5] in any event because, although people were perfectly nice to me when I played at the club in a city tournament, I was just as happy to get away between rounds. There was a polite frostiness about the whole place that made me quite reconciled[6] to going back and playing on the municipal course.

Actually a short while later it turned out not to matter that I didn't have the advantage of being able to use the club course. When I became amateur state champion, the mayor of the city not only gave me free use of my old friend, the municipal course, but also free golf privileges on another infinitely[7] better city golf course, located on a military school's grounds right there in Roswell. So I got plenty of good golf play from then on, without the frills.

[4] not practical or useful

[5] environment; surroundings

[6] accepting or resigned

[7] vastly; greatly

[8] conforming to accepted
standards; customary

[9] ask; question

[10] a champion
professional golfer

[11] examine in detail

I sometimes wonder what would have happened if a teaching professional from a country club had latched onto me at that stage. My Dad left my natural game alone, but I don't know if a pro could have resisted taking me apart and putting me together again, because I know that my swing is regarded as neither conventional[8] nor stylish. But I felt comfortable with it and still do, particularly ever since the time I had a chance to query[9] a fellow Mexican American, Lee Trevino,[10] about it. I said, "Mr. Trevino, what should I do about my golf swing? I have a bad golf swing and yet I play very well."

Trevino didn't ask me to show him my swing at all. Instead he simply said, "You can't argue with success. If you swing badly but still score well and win, don't change a thing."

That was quite a while back but I never forgot what he said and so far, at least, he's turned out to be right. The less I analyze[11] my swing, the better off I believe myself to be. I will think about aspects of my game, like keeping my cool and concentrating when the chips are down, but except when putting (which is a separate game) I don't worry about the mechanics of a stroke. I do what Dad taught me: "Come up on the backswing real slow and real high, extend, and hit the ball."

About the Author

Nancy Lopez, a professional golfer, won both Rookie and Player of the Year Awards in 1978. She has had dozens of victories in the world of professional golf. In addition to her autobiography, Lopez has written *The Complete Golfer*.

Responding to the Autobiography

▼ Think Back

What obstacles did Nancy Lopez overcome?

How did Lee Trevino's advice change Nancy's approach to her golf game?

Why does Nancy have mixed feelings about her hometown of Roswell, New Mexico?

▼ Discuss

Nancy's father gave her Barbie dolls as rewards for winning golf tournaments. What other kinds of incentives are used to motivate athletes? Are any inappropriate?

Lee Trevino's advice to Nancy is a variation on the saying, "If it isn't broken, don't fix it." Do you agree or disagree with this statement? Why?

▼ Write

Find Quotations Lopez uses direct quotations to support important ideas. By using her father's exact words, "Nancy win. Nancy get every doll in the shop!" she introduces the fact that he and she are Mexican Americans. Copy other direct quotations from the selection. Note how each supports Lopez's ideas.

Write an Essay Think about one of your hobbies or athletic skills. What important lessons have you learned? Who taught you? Write a brief essay describing a learning experience. Use direct quotations.

Grassy's Theme

Jesse Stuart

When Jesse Stuart was a high school teacher, Grassy was his student. What makes Grassy the kind of student a teacher can't forget?

His name was Bruce Barnhill, but the pupils called him "Grassy" because he and his sister Daisy were the only ones who walked the eight miles from Grassy Valley to McKell High School in South Shore from 1932 to 1936.

Grassy was six-feet-two, with fair skin, large blue eyes, and a shock of hair as golden as ripe wheat stems. Daisy could have passed for his twin, except that she wasn't as tall. Although a year older than he, she was in the same class.

What made me remember Grassy was a theme he wrote for my English class when he was a senior. One day a week my students wrote on any topic they chose, then read their themes aloud. Grassy's theme was about jumping up and cracking his heels together. Because he was interested in math, time, space, and the universe, he wondered why the earth didn't move from under him when he jumped up and cracked his heels together.

He had practiced jumping so that he could stay in the air long enough to crack his heels together two and sometimes three times, and he had his sister Daisy time him with a stopwatch to see how long he was in the air on each jump.

The subject of Grassy's theme dealt with where he figured he should have been when he landed on the ground after his jumps. Using figures based on the rotation[1] of the earth in space and time, he showed that when he cracked his heels together once in the McKell High School yard he should have come to earth in Fairlington, Kentucky, and after he had cracked them twice he should have landed on the west side of Portsmouth, Ohio.

[1] movement around an axis

When Grassy was reading his theme to the class he looked up from his paper partway through to see how the other students were reacting. They were smiling. Grassy had a hot temper, and he obviously didn't like those smiles.

"Read on," I said quickly. "This is a very interesting theme."

Grassy's face was flushed as he began to read the last part of his theme, which discussed where he should have landed after cracking his heels together three times in the air. According to his calculations,[2] he should have come to earth on the western border of Sinton County, Ohio. He closed his theme by saying he hadn't been able to figure out why his experiments hadn't worked.

[2] mathematical figuring

Twenty-three students exploded in laughter. They couldn't hold back any longer. Grassy's temper flared.

He was ready to start swinging when I hurried over and put my hand on his shoulder. He was trembling like a dry sassafras leaf in a September wind.

"That's the most interesting theme that's been read in this English class," I said. "Now, of course, I don't know about your figures. I'm not good enough in math to follow you."

"The figures are correct," he said, still trembling, "but I can't understand why I dropped back every jump to the same place where I was standing when I jumped."

"There is a thing called gravity that held you in place," I said.

Now he smiled, and his classmates stopped laughing. They looked at Grassy with puzzled expressions on their faces.

"How long have you been working on this theme?" I asked.

"I've been thinking about it ever since last year," he replied. "This year it's taken weeks for me to practice my jumps and for Daisy to get the timing. I had to figure my distances too, before I could write the theme."

He handed me pages of figures to back up what he had written.

"I've never had anybody work harder and longer on one theme or put more thought into it than you did on this one," I told him. "It's the most original idea I've ever had a student write about."

I gave him the only A plus I had given the class and showed my gradebook to the students. Grassy smiled faintly; then his face became serious. "Gravity," he sighed, "gravity."

Later I took Grassy's theme and his calculations to one of the math teachers and asked her to see if the figures were correct.

"Bruce is a genius with figures," she said. "If they're his calculations, I'm almost sure they're right, but I'll go over them for you."

Two days later she reported that Grassy's calculations were correct.

"Did his theme interest you?" I asked.

"The beauty in his calculations interested me more. There's lots of work behind every sentence of his theme. But his kind of thinking is a little crazy, isn't it?"

"I like his kind of thinking," I said. "He may never put it to any practical use, but he's certainly original."

"It doesn't make good sense. He ought to know, smart as he is, that people have jumped in the air before, and the earth didn't spin under them. I hope he can keep his feet on the ground!"

Now, I have remembered Grassy all my life just for that one theme. But as it happens, this story has a sequel[3] that will show you how a teacher can sometimes be wrong in his estimate of a pupil.

[3] follow-up

In due course, Grassy and Daisy graduated and went to teacher's college. I heard that they were making A's and that Grassy was a track star.

In 1937 I left Greenwood to go to work on a fellowship, and when I returned I taught in Portsmouth,

Ohio. I didn't hear any more about the Barnhills until one summer day in 1940, when I was back in Greenwood, and I met their father, Eif, on the street. He greeted me with a smile and a friendly handshake.

"I wanted to tell you that Daisy and Grassy finished college," he said. "There were over three hundred in the graduating class, and Grassy finished first and Daisy second."

"Where are they now?"

"Daisy is teaching at Plum Fork School," he replied. "And Grassy, well, he went to California."

"Is he teaching in California?"

"Ah, Grassy . . . " he stammered. "He's still in California. When he writes, he never says anything about his work."

"No, he's not teaching. He never tells us about what he's doing in his letters, but I think he's working in a factory."

In 1941, when the United States began fighting a war on two fronts, I enlisted in the navy. Years passed—1942, 1943, 1944. While I was home on leave at Christmas in 1944, I met Eif Barnhill again. I asked about Daisy and Grassy. He told me proudly that Daisy was teaching in a big high school in Nebraska.

"And Grassy?" I asked. "What branch of the service is he in?"

"Ah, Grassy . . ." he stammered. "He's still in California. When he writes, he never says anything about his work." Eif's face was flushed, and he looked away from me.

"I can't blame you for feeling embarrassed," I thought. "Your son was the best physical specimen[4] in McKell High, yet as far as I know he's the only one of all the boys in his graduating class who's not in the service."

[4] an individual representative of a group or class

In the years that followed, I tried to keep from thinking about Grassy, but I never could forget him. Since he had never come home, I wondered if his hot temper got him into a fight that had landed him in prison.

In 1956 I returned to South Shore as principal of McKell High. One October morning a sunburned blond youth of about fourteen came into my office. When I looked at him, it was like looking at the Grassy Barnhill of twenty years before. Seeing him brought a strange, unpleasant feeling to me.

"Sir, did you used to teach Bruce Barnhill?" he asked. "Everybody called him Grassy."

"Yes, I did," I replied to the smiling boy.

"He's my cousin," he said. "My father is his father's youngest brother. Do you know where he is now?"

"In prison," I thought, but I didn't tell the boy what I was thinking.

"The last I knew he was in California," I said. "He's been transferred."

I looked at this image of Grassy, who beamed with pride when he spoke of his cousin.

"He's at Cape Canaveral now," he said. "He's one of the high men working on missile[5] projects down there."

Suddenly I understood many things. Now I was beaming with as much pride as his young cousin. "Well, Grassy," I said to myself, "you have certainly jumped higher and cracked your heels together more than three times."

[5] space rocket

About the Author

Jesse Stuart (1906–1984) was born in Greenup County, Kentucky, where he served as a teacher, high school principal, and county school superintendent—a job he earned at the age of 23. His teaching experiences inspired his book *The Thread That Runs So True* (1949). Though a world traveler, Stuart never forgot his roots in rural Kentucky. He died in 1984 and was buried in Plum Grove Cemetery in Greenup County.

Responding to the Story

Think Back

What made Grassy so different or unusual?

Why didn't Grassy tell anybody about his work in California?

In what ways did Grassy Barnhill affect Jesse Stuart?

Discuss

Do you agree with Grassy's math teacher, who said Grassy's thinking is a little crazy? Or do you agree with Stuart, who liked Grassy's thinking? Explain.

What did you learn from reading about Grassy Barnhill's life?

Write

Write Dialogue Notice how Jesse Stuart uses dialogue, people's exact words, to show the reader how the events in "Grassy's Theme" actually happened and what the people were really like. Imagine that Grassy Barnhill visited Stuart thirty years after he graduated. Write a conversation between the two.

Write an Essay Think about a memorable person you met once and have never seen since. What was so memorable about the meeting or about the person? Write a short essay about that event. Use dialogue to make your story more realistic.

Martin Luther King Jr.

Gwendolyn Brooks

Martin Luther King, Jr., a great civil rights leader, led a march on Washington, D.C., in August 1963. There he delivered his famous "I Have a Dream" speech to hundreds of thousands of Americans, black and white, who gathered to show support for equal rights. Gwendolyn Brooks's poem is a tribute to this man and to his ideals.

[1] to put or rub oil on

[2] barriers; obstructions

A man went forth with gifts.

He was a prose poem.
He was a tragic grace.
He was a warm music.

He tried to heal the vivid volcanoes.
His ashes are
    reading the world.

His Dream still wishes to anoint[1]
    the barricades[2] of faith and of control.

His word still burns the center of the sun,
    above the thousands and the
    hundred thousands.

The word was Justice. It was spoken.

So it shall be spoken.
So it shall be done.

Responding to the Poem

▼ Think Back

How does Gwendolyn Brooks describe Martin Luther King, Jr.?

To which senses does Brooks appeal in this poem?

▼ Discuss

Why does Brooks capitalize the words *Dream* and *Justice*?

Where do Brooks and King want justice imposed?

Why do you think Gwendolyn Brooks wrote this poem?

▼ Write

Analyze Metaphors A metaphor is a figure of speech in which two unlike objects are compared without using the words *like* or *as*. Reread the poem to identify the metaphors. Write an explanation of the comparisons. Discuss whether the metaphors are effective.

Write a Poem Think about someone you greatly admire and respect. Using "Martin Luther King Jr." as a guide, write a poem about that person. Create several metaphors to illustrate why that person is special.

About the Author

Gwendolyn Brooks was the first African American to receive the Pulitzer Prize for poetry (1950, *Annie Allen*). Brooks says that she writes "*to* African Americans, *for* anyone who wants to open the book."

Opera, Karate, and Bandits

Huynh Quang Nhuong

We often stereotype grandmothers as sweet little old ladies. This author's grandmother definitely does not fit that description.

[1] decreased; lessened

[2] very small village

When she was eighty years old my grandmother was still quite strong. She could use her own teeth to eat corn on the cob or to chew on sugar plants to extract juice from them. Every two days she walked for more than an hour to reach the marketplace, carrying a heavy load of food with her, and then spent another hour walking back home. And even though she was quite old, traces of her beauty still lingered on: Her hands, her feet, her face revealed that she had been an attractive young woman. Nor did time do much damage to the youthful spirit of my grandmother.

One of her great passions was theater, and this passion never diminished[1] with age. No matter how busy she was, she never missed a show when there was a group of actors in town. If no actors visited our hamlet[2] for several months, she would organize her own show in which she was the manager, the producer, and the young leading lady, all at the same time.

My grandmother's own plays were always melodramas[3] inspired by books she had read and by what she had seen on the stage. She always chose her favorite grandson to play the role of the hero, who would, without fail, marry the heroine at the end and live happily ever after. And when my sisters would tell her that she was getting too old to play the role of the young heroine anymore, my grandmother merely replied: "Anybody can play this role if she's young at heart."

When I was a little boy my grandmother often took me to see the opera. She knew Chinese mythology by heart, and the opera was often a dramatization of this mythology. On one special occasion, during the Lunar New Year celebrations—my favorite holiday, because children could do anything they wanted and by tradition no one could scold them—I accompanied my grandmother to the opera.

When we reached the theater I wanted to go in immediately. But my grandmother wanted to linger at the entrance and talk to her friends. She chatted for more than an hour. Finally we entered the theater, and at that moment the "Faithful One" was onstage, singing sadly. The "Faithful One" is a common character in Chinese opera. He could be a good minister, or a valiant[4] general, or someone who loved and served his king faithfully. But in the end he is unjustly persecuted[5] by the king, whose opinion of him has been changed by the lies of the "Flatterer," another standard character.

When my grandmother saw the "Faithful One" onstage she looked upset and gave a great sigh. I was too

[3] plays with exaggerated conflicts and emotions

[4] brave

[5] cruelly treated

interested in what was happening to ask her the reason, and we spent the next five hours watching the rest of the opera. Sometimes I cried because my grandmother cried at the pitiful situation of the "Faithful One." Sometimes I became as angry as my grandmother did at the wickedness of the "Flatterer."

The kick was so swift that my grandfather didn't even see it. He only heard a heavy thud, and then saw the rascal tumble backward and collapse on the ground.

When we went home that night my grandmother was quite sad. She told my mother that she would have bad luck in the following year because when we entered the theater, the "Faithful One" was onstage. I was puzzled. I told my grandmother that she was confused. It would be a good year for us because we saw the good guy first. But my mother said, "No, son. The 'Faithful One' always is in trouble and it takes him many years to vindicate[6] himself. Our next year is going to be like one of his bad years."

So, according to my mother's and grandmother's logic, we would have been much better off in the new year if we had been lucky enough to see the villain first!

✳ ✳ ✳

[6] to clear from blame and criticism

My grandmother had married a man whom she loved with all her heart, but who was totally different from her. My grandfather was very shy, never laughed loudly, and always spoke very softly. And physically he was not as strong as my grandmother. But he excused his lack of physical strength by saying that he was a "scholar."

About three months after their marriage, my grandparents were in a restaurant and a rascal began to insult my grandfather because he looked weak and had a pretty wife. At first he just made insulting remarks, such as, "Hey! Wet chicken! This is no place for a weakling!"

My grandfather wanted to leave the restaurant even though he and my grandmother had not yet finished their meal. But my grandmother pulled his shirt sleeve and signaled him to remain seated. She continued to eat and looked as if nothing had happened.

Tired of yelling insults without any result, the rascal got up from his table, moved over to my grandparents' table, and grabbed my grandfather's chopsticks. My grandmother immediately wrested the chopsticks from him and struck the rascal on his cheekbone with her elbow. The blow was so quick and powerful that he lost his balance and fell on the floor. Instead of finishing him off, as any street fighter would do, my grandmother let the rascal recover from the blow. But as soon as he got up again, he kicked over the table between him and my grandmother, making food and drink fly all over the place. Before he could do anything else, my grandmother kicked him on the chin. The kick was so swift that my grandfather didn't even see it. He only heard a heavy thud, and then saw the rascal tumble backward and collapse on the ground.

All the onlookers were surprised and delighted, especially the owner of the restaurant. Apparently the rascal, one of the best karate fighters of our area, came to his restaurant every day and left without paying for his food or drink, but the owner was too afraid to confront him.

While the rascal's friends tried to revive him, everyone else surrounded my grandmother and asked her who had taught her karate. She said, "Who else? My husband!"

After the fight at the restaurant people assumed that my grandfather knew karate very well but refused to use it for fear of killing someone. In reality, my grandmother had received special training in karate from my great-great uncle from the time she was eight years old.

Anyway, after that incident, my grandfather never had to worry again. Anytime he had business downtown, people treated him very well. And whenever anyone happened to bump into him on the street, they bowed to my grandfather in a very respectful way.

＊ ＊ ＊

When my father was about ten years old a group of bandits attacked our house. There had been a very poor harvest that year, and bandits had already attacked several homes in other hamlets. My grandmother had a premonition[7] this would also happen to them, so she devised a plan. In case of danger, she would carry the

[7] a feeling that something will happen

children to safety, and my grandfather would carry the bow and arrows, a bottle of poison, and the box containing the family jewels.

It was night when the bandits came. My grandfather became scared to death and forgot his part of the plan, but my grandmother remained very calm. She led her husband and children to safety through a secret back door that opened into a double hedge of cactus that allowed a person to walk inside, undetected, to the banana grove. When they were safely inside the banana grove, my grandfather realized that he had forgotten the bow and arrows and the bottle of poison. So my grandmother stole back into the house and retrieved[8] the weapons.

[8] saved; rescued

The bandits were still trying to smash through our very solid front door when she sneaked out of the house for the second time. She dipped one arrow in poison and crawled around to the front of the house near the bandits. But, upon second thought, she put the poisoned arrow aside and took another arrow and carefully aimed at the leg of the bandit leader. When the arrow hit his thigh the bandit let out a loud cry and fell backward.

The night was so dark that none of the bandits knew where the arrow had come from. And moments later, friends started arriving and began to attack them from the road in front of our house. The bandits panicked and left in a hurry. But my grandmother spent the rest of the night with her family in the banana grove, just in case the bandits came back.

✳ ✳ ✳

When my grandmother became older she felt sick once in a while. Before the arrival of the doctor, she would order everybody in the house to look sad. And during the consultation[9] with the doctor she acted as if she were much sicker than she really was. My grandmother felt that she had to make herself look really sick so that the doctor would give her good medicine. She told the doctor that she had a pain in the head, in the shoulders, in the chest, in the back, in the limbs—pain everywhere. Finally the doctor would become confused and wouldn't know what could be wrong with her.

Whenever the doctor left, my mother would sneak out of the house, meet him at the other side of the garden, and tell him exactly where my grandmother hurt.

[9] a meeting to talk over a situation

She told the doctor that she had a pain in the head, in the shoulders, in the chest, in the back, in the limbs—pain everywhere.

Two or three days later my grandmother usually felt much better. But before the doctor arrived for another visit she ordered us to look sad again—not as sad as the first time, but quite sad. She would tell the doctor that her situation had improved a little bit but that she still felt quite sick. My grandmother thought that if she told the doctor she had been feeling much better he would stop giving her good medicine. When the doctor left my mother sneaked out of the house again and informed him of the real condition of my grandmother.

I don't think my grandmother ever guessed it was my mother's reports to the doctor, and not her acting, that helped her get well.

❋ ❋ ❋

One morning my grandmother wanted me to go outside with her. We climbed a little hill that looked over the whole area, and when we got to the top she looked at the rice field below, the mountain on the horizon, and especially at the river. As a young girl she had often brought her herd of water buffaloes to the river to drink while she swam with the other children of the village. Then we visited the graveyard where her husband and some of her children were buried. She touched her husband's tombstone and said, "Dear, I will join you soon." And then we walked back to the garden and she gazed at the fruit trees her husband had planted, a new one for each time she had given birth to a child. Finally, before we left the garden my sister joined us, and the two of them fed a few ducks swimming in the pond.

That evening my grandmother did not eat much of her dinner. After dinner she combed her hair and put on her best dress. We thought that she was going to go out again, but instead she went to her bedroom and told us that she didn't want to be disturbed.

The family dog seemed to sense something was amiss,[10] for he kept looking anxiously at everybody and whined from time to time. At midnight my mother went to my grandmother's room and found that she had died, with her eyes shut, as if she were sleeping normally.

It took me a long time to get used to the reality that my grandmother had passed away. Wherever I was, in the house, in the garden, out on the fields, her face always appeared so clearly to me. And even now, many years later, I still have the feeling that my last conversation with her has happened only a few days before.

About the Author

Huynh Quang Nhuong was born in Vietnam and pursued a career in chemistry. While serving in the South Vietnamese army, he became paralyzed from a gunshot wound. In 1969 he came to the United States for medical treatment and stayed to earn degrees in French and literature. "Opera, Karate, and Bandits" is an excerpt from *The Land I Lost*, Mr. Huynh's first book, a collection of stories and memories of his Vietnamese childhood.

Responding to the Story

▼ Think Back

What are some things the narrator's grandmother could do at the age of eighty?

Why did the narrator's grandmother and mother think that seeing the "Faithful One" onstage upon entering the theater was bad luck?

How did the grandmother deal with the rascal in the restaurant? How did she deal with the bandits?

▼ Discuss

What was the narrator's grandmother like? With your class, make a list of words or phrases that describe the grandmother. Explain your word choices.

Have you ever known somebody like the narrator's grandmother—a person who greatly influenced your life? Describe that person.

▼ Write

Write a Scene Huynh Quang Nhuong's grandmother wrote her own plays. Choose an incident from her life and write a scene for a play about it. Write the words the characters are to say next to each character's name. Write stage directions in parentheses.

Write a Summary The author related many incidents about his grandmother. Based on this information, write a one-paragraph summary describing her character.

Theme Links

Special People

In this unit, you've read about special people—people who have affected others' lives. You have also discussed and thought about the special people in your life and how they have influenced you.

▼ Group Discussion

With a partner or in a small group, talk about the selections in this unit and how they relate to the theme and to your own lives. Use questions like the following to guide the discussion.

- What is special about each of the people profiled in the selections in this unit?
- What qualities or personality traits do many of the "special" people in the selections share?
- What can you do to change other people's lives for the better or to have a positive effect on your family or friends?

▼ Advice from a Panel of Experts

With a group of classmates, form a panel made up of Nancy Lopez's father, Martin Luther King, Jr., Grassy Barnhill, Grandma Ling, and Grandma Traub. Choose roles and have each panel member give a short presentation about how to be an inspiration to others. Panel members should use examples from their own lives to illustrate their points.

▼ Special People

In your exploration of the theme, you've discovered that many "special" people are average citizens: family members, teachers, neighbors. What family members, teachers, or citizens in your community have made a difference in your life or in the lives of others? Create a poster dedicated to one of these special people. Your poster might include:

- the name and an introduction of the special person
- a photograph or portrait
- descriptions or photographs of his or her achievements
- quotations from the person
- quotations from people whose lives were touched by this person

Make a community hall of fame. Ask permission to hang your posters in a well-traveled area of your school for everyone to see.

▼ The Theme and You

Write a biographical sketch about a special person in your life. After a brief description of the person's life, explain why the person is so special to you.

Food for
Thought

Like water and air, food is one of the necessities
of life—everyone needs it. Food is an important
part of many holidays and other social and cultural
celebrations.

Food also plays a part in many pieces of literature.
It can help authors set a scene or show a mood. The
authors of the selections in this unit use food to
illustrate cultural differences, to talk about childhood
memories, and to comment on trends in modern
society.

As you read these selections, think about each
author's purpose for writing. Think about the
associations food has for you. What is your favorite
food? Where and when do you like to eat? What
memories do you associate with certain foods?
Also think about how each selection provides
"food for thought."

How to Eat a Guava

E s m e r a l d a   S a n t i a g o

The sight, touch, and smell of a guava trigger Esmeralda Santiago's memories of her childhood in Puerto Rico.

[1] narrow spaces

T here are guavas at the Shop & Save. I pick one the size of a tennis ball and finger the prickly stem end. It feels familiarly bumpy and firm. The guava is not quite ripe; the skin is still a dark green. I smell it and imagine a pale pink center, the seeds tightly embedded in the flesh.

A ripe guava is yellow, although some varieties have a pink tinge. The skin is thick, firm, and sweet. Its heart is bright pink and almost solid with seeds. The most delicious part of the guava surrounds the tiny seeds. If you don't know how to eat a guava, the seeds end up in the crevices[1] between your teeth.

When you bite into a ripe guava, your teeth must grip the bumpy surface and sink into the thick edible skin without hitting the center. It takes experience to do this, as it's quite tricky to determine how far beyond the skin the seeds begin.

Some years, when the rains have been plentiful and the nights cool, you can bite into a guava and not find many seeds. The guava bushes grow close to the ground, their branches laden with green then yellow fruit that seem to ripen overnight. These guavas are large and juicy, almost seedless, their roundness enticing[2] you to have one more, just one more, because next year the rains may not come.

2 tempting

As children, we didn't always wait for the fruit to ripen. We raided the bushes as soon as the guavas were large enough to bend the branch.

A green guava is sour and hard. You bite into it at its widest point, because it's easier to grasp with your teeth. You hear the skin, meat, and seeds crunching inside your head, while the inside of your mouth explodes in little spurts of sour.

You grimace,[3] your eyes water, and your cheeks disappear as your lips purse into a tight O. But you have another and then another, enjoying the crunchy sounds, the acid taste, the gritty texture of the unripe center. At night, your mother makes you drink castor oil, which she says tastes better than a green guava. That's when you know for sure that you're a child and she has stopped being one.

3 to show a look of pain or disgust

I had my last guava the day we left Puerto Rico. It was large and juicy, almost red in the center, and so fragrant that I didn't want to eat it because I would lose the smell. All the way to the airport I scratched at it with my teeth, making little dents in the skin, chewing small pieces with my front teeth, so that I could feel the texture against my tongue, the tiny pink pellets[4] of sweet.

4 small ball-shaped pieces

Today, I stand before a stack of dark green guavas, each perfectly round and hard, each $1.59. The one in my hand is tempting. It smells faintly of late summer afternoons and hopscotch under the mango tree. But this is autumn in New York, and I'm no longer a child.

The guava joins its sisters under the harsh fluorescent lights of the exotic[5] fruit display. I push my cart away, toward the apples and pears of my adulthood, their nearly seedless ripeness predictable and bittersweet.[6]

[5] strikingly different or unusual

[6] being bitter and sweet at the same time; pleasant, but with elements of pain

About the Author

Esmeralda Santiago was born in Puerto Rico. When she was thirteen, she and her family moved to New York City. A very determined child, the oldest of eleven children, she won admittance to the High School of Performing Arts and later to Harvard University, where she graduated with honors. Her works have appeared in the *New York Times*, the *Boston Globe*, and the *Christian Science Monitor*. "How to Eat a Guava" is an excerpt from Santiago's first book, *When I Was Puerto Rican*.

Responding to the Essay

▼ **Think Back**

Where is the author from? Where does she live now?

What effect does seeing the guava in the store have on Santiago?

Does Esmeralda Santiago like or dislike guavas? What details give you clues to her feelings?

▼ **Discuss**

Why do you think Santiago hasn't eaten a guava since leaving Puerto Rico?

Is there a food that brings back memories of your childhood? What is it, and what are the memories?

Why does Santiago, as an adult, prefer the "predictable and bittersweet" ripeness of apples and pears?

▼ **Write**

Use Sensory Details Did you get hungry while reading "How to Eat a Guava"? Reread Esmeralda Santiago's description of eating a green guava to see how she uses sensory language. Then try your hand at creating vivid sensory language by describing a favorite food and what it feels like to eat it.

Make a Menu Menu writers use sensory details to describe foods. Make a menu for a restaurant that serves all of your favorite foods. Use sensory details to make the food sound mouth-wateringly delicious.

In My Mother's Kitchen

Shonto Begay

Is your kitchen a quiet place, or is it full of noise and clutter? Shonto Begay lovingly describes his mother in her kitchen.

Fragrance[1] of fresh tortillas and corn stew

Fills my mother's kitchen

Sparsely[2] furnished

Crowded with warmth

Soot-grayed walls, secretive and blank

She moves gently in and out of light

Like a dream just out of reach

The morning light gives her a halo

That plays upon her crown of dark hair

Strong brown hands caress soft mounds of dough

She gazes out into the warming day

Past sagebrush[3] hills, out towards the foot of Black Mesa

How far would she let the goats wander today

Before it rains

[1] a pleasant smell

[2] barely; having less than usual

[3] a plant common in dry areas of the western United States

Childhood dreams and warmth

Tight in my throat, tears in my eyes

The radio softly tuned to a local AM station

News of ceremonies and chapter meetings

And funerals

Flows into the peaceful kitchen

Lines upon her face, features carved of hard times

Lines around her eyes, creases of happy times

Bittersweet tears and ringing silvery laughter

I ache in my heart

My mother's gentle movements light up dark corners

Her gentle smiles recall childhood dreams still so alive

My mother moves in and out of light

Like clouds on days of promising rain

About the Author

Shonto Begay was born in a hogan near Shonto, Arizona, the fifth of sixteen children of a Navajo medicine man. He studied fine arts and has had more than thirty exhibitions of his works. He wrote and illustrated _NAVAJO Visions and Voices Across the Mesa_—in which this poem appears—a collection of deeply personal poems and paintings. Begay's picture book _Ma'ii and Cousin Horned Toad_ won a 1993 Arizona Author Award.

Responding to the Poem

▼ Think Back

What is the setting of this poem? What details give you clues about the location of the house?

How does the speaker feel about his mother?

What emotions does the speaker describe in this poem?

▼ Discuss

In your opinion, why might the speaker have a tightness in his throat, tears in his eyes, and an ache in his heart?

There are contrasting images in this poem—some warm and comforting, others cold and somber. How does the poem make you feel?

What is the key ingredient in the childhood kitchen of Shonto Begay? Explain.

▼ Write

Respond to Imagery There are many vivid sensory images in this poem. Reread it to identify an image that you find especially effective. Then write a brief explanation of why you find that image so memorable.

Write a Poem Is there a special kitchen or other room that you remember from your childhood? What images come to mind when you think about it? Write a poem that describes the room, using vivid images to recapture how it looks and to express your feelings about it.

A Taste of Korea

M a r i e   G .   L e e

Yoon Jun, a Korean immigrant, hopes to make friends at his new school. Alice, the only other Korean student there, was adopted as a baby by the Larsens, who urge her to be friendly to Yoon Jun. Alice reluctantly agrees to work with him to present Korean food at the school's International Day. Yoon Jun invites her to his apartment to taste the food his mother has prepared.

Besides tasting foods that are new to her, what else does Alice find out about her native culture?

You want to use fork, or chopsticks?" asked Yoon Jun.

"Fork," said Alice. The only time she'd ever used chopsticks was when she and her family had gone to a Chinese restaurant, but she hadn't been able to get the hang of it.

Alice warily[1] took a bite of the pancake. It was fluffy, almost eggy, and didn't taste like much.

"Here," said Mrs. Lee. "You can put some soy sauce on it." She handed Alice a tiny bowl that had soy sauce with pieces of green onion floating on top. Alice

[1] cautiously

put some of that on, took another bite, and then tasted mostly salt.

"How you like it?" Mrs. Lee asked anxiously.

"Very good," said Alice. Of course she would rather have macaroni and cheese, but it wasn't too bad, really.

"Good," said Mrs. Lee, turning the dial of the griddle. "Now, we try another favorite Korean dish, *bulkoki*."

While the griddle heated, she spooned out some rice for everyone. This rice was sticky, and not as long-grained as the Minute Rice they had at home.

When the griddle started to smoke, Mrs. Lee brought out the bowl of meat—it *was* raw meat. She threw it and the bowls of mushrooms, spinach, and bean sprouts onto the hot surface. The meat, Alice noticed, was cut almost paper-thin, so it started turning from red to brown right away.

Merrily, Mrs. Lee stirred everything around as a cloud of smoke and steam rose from it. Alice smelled sizzling meat, ginger, and sesame. To her surprise, her mouth started to water.

Mrs. Lee ceremoniously[2] lifted a clump of cooked meat and vegetables with her chopsticks and deposited it onto Alice's clean, white rice.

"And this," said Mrs. Lee, taking out some pink, suspicious-looking vegetable from a jar, "is Korea's national treasure, *kimchee*."

"What is it?" asked Alice, uneasily.

"Cabbage and spice, mainly," she said. "I just give you a small bit in case you not like it."

[2] in a formal way

Alice looked down at the wilted leaf on her plate. This was the big deal they named that Korean camp in Brainerd after?

She tried the meat first because it looked safer. It was actually pretty good: soy-saucy and a little sweet. The vegetables had fried up crispy and delicious.

Alice looked over at Yoon Jun, who was shoveling food into his mouth as though he hadn't eaten in years. He made funny sucking noises as he ate—almost like oinking sounds. Alice shuddered slightly.

"Yoon Jun is telling me that he likes my cooking," said Mrs. Lee, catching Alice's gaze. Alice felt instantly embarrassed.

"In Korea," she went on, "you tell the cook you like her food by eating with lots of noise."

"Really? If I ate that way at home, my parents would kill me," Alice couldn't help saying.

Mrs. Lee smiled wisely. "Ah, Korean and American customs not always coincide.[3] I am glad to learn more about American culture from you."

Alice was feeling more embarrassed by the minute. The Lees were obviously very poor, and here she was barging in and eating their food, and then acting as though Yoon Jun had bad manners.

The *kimchee* had been sitting forlornly[4] on her plate for a while, so Alice finally lifted it up. It was mottled with angry red spices, and the pungent[5] smell of vinegar tickled her nose. *Here goes nothing*, she thought, and she dropped the limp leaf into her mouth.

[3] agree or be exactly alike

[4] in a sad and lonely way

[5] sharp

It was surprisingly crunchy, and spicy, and weird-tasting. But the more she chewed, the more she wanted to taste that sharp taste again, even though it stung her mouth. Soon, she had cleaned all the pieces off her plate.

"You like?" Mrs. Lee beamed.

"Yes," said Alice, holding her plate up for more. It wasn't exactly that the taste was good, it was more addictive.

"*Kimchee* is what makes Koreans so healthy," Mrs. Lee announced. "It is full of good things—hot peppers and garlic."

Garlic? thought Alice. She hated garlic. She hated it when she smelled it in Yoon Jun's lunch. Was he carrying *kimchee*?

Still, she couldn't help eating some more. It didn't taste all that garlicky to her. Mostly, it just tasted hot.

After dinner, Mrs. Lee served a warm, sweet tea that had grains of rice at the bottom. She also brought out the chocolates.

"Ah, chocolate," she said with relish. "This is one of the things I like best about America."

A little later, Mrs. Lee excused herself, and Alice saw her disappear into one of the small rooms down the hall. If that was the bathroom, the other must be the bedroom, she thought.

"Where is your room?" Alice inquired politely to Yoon Jun. He saw her looking down the hall.

"Over there." He pointed in the direction Alice was looking. "I share with my mother."

"What?" Alice said, sure she couldn't have heard right.

"I share room with my mother," he repeated.

Alice was astounded. "Don't you miss your privacy?"

"What for I need privacy?" he said. "We just sleep in there, and I like my mother. She don't snore or anything."

"But I'd go crazy if I had to sleep with my parents," said Alice. "Just knowing they were there."

Yoon Jun laughed. "You kidding? In Seoul, our whole family practically live in one room—me with all my cousins, and they snore and kick."

"Does everyone in Korea live like that?" Alice asked.

"Oh no," he said. "But Seoul very crowded. People have to grow gardens on top of buildings."

"Why would anyone want to live in Seoul?"

"My father had a job in a bank," Yoon Jun said, and Alice saw his face turn sad. "Before he died, he had a very good job in a bank, and best jobs all in Seoul."

Alice wanted to ask him more about his father, and about why he and his mother came to the United States. But she suddenly realized how grateful she was that Yoon Jun and his mother weren't prying at her with a bunch of pesky questions about what it was like being adopted, did she have any idea what her Korean mother was like or why she gave her up—all those questions that rude people seemed to like to ask when they first met her.

Mrs. Lee returned to the table and sipped the rest of her rice tea thoughtfully. "You like *kimchee*, yes?" she asked Alice.

"Yes, I do," Alice answered sincerely.

Mrs. Lee broke into a smile. "Good," she said. "Then I will put some in a jar for you. Maybe mother and father would like to try, too."

"Oh, that's very nice of you," said Alice quickly. The Lees seemed so poor—she didn't want to take what little food they had. "But you don't have to do that. It was already so nice of you to share this dinner with me."

"If you like," Mrs. Lee said, smiling with satisfaction, "then perhaps mother and father will like, too." She excused herself from the table, and Alice could hear the clinking of a jar.

"Your mom is awfully nice," Alice said to Yoon Jun, low.

"Yes," Yoon Jun agreed. "She likes to give of herself. Now, you think this food okay to serve at school?"

"More than okay," Alice said. "Do you need me to get anything from the grocery store?"

"Oh no, don't worry," he said.

Mrs. Lee returned with a jar full of *kimchee*. "Now, you make sure to give mother and father a taste," she said with a laugh.

In some ways, Alice was almost sad to leave the apartment. Before, Mrs. Lee and Yoon Jun had seemed so foreign, but now, strangely, they seemed almost familiar.

She was thinking back to what Laura had asked: Did she have any memories of Korea? She didn't. Babies don't remember things. But she had read somewhere that people thought babies could hear things while still in their mothers' bellies.

Could that be possible? She didn't understand a single word of Korean, but when Yoon Jun and his mother were speaking that singing language to each other, Alice knew she had heard those sounds before. She *knew* it.

The few times Alice had even thought about Korea, she always fantasized that her mother was a beautiful Korean princess—if they had princesses in Korea—and that her father was a prince or something. Sometimes she imagined that her mother was a blue-eyed blonde who had to give Alice up because the royal family of her husband, the Korean king, objected, and one day she would wake up to find that the blonde genes had taken over.

That's what she would like best, she decided, to be able to blend in completely with her family. To be blonde like Mary. But as she thought this, she couldn't ignore the sounds of Korean words beating like far-off drums in her head.

At dinner the next night, Alice let everyone try the *kimchee.*

"What's this?" said her father. "Korean pickles?"

"Pickled cabbage," said Alice. "It's called *kimchee.* Mrs. Lee said it's one of Korea's national treasures."

Mrs. Larsen eyed the jar uneasily. She took a sniff. "My," she said. "It sure smells spicy."

"Looks ucky," concluded Mary.

"Now, don't call anything ucky until you've tried it," said Reverend Larsen. To set an example, he fished out a rather large piece of it and deposited it into his mouth, without smelling it or anything. He coughed once as he chewed.

"Mmm," he said, through his beard. "This is quite good."

He took another piece. Alice's mother sliced a small piece off of that and ate it. Her eyes grew wide as she did. "I was right," she said. "It *is* spicy."

"Here, Mare," Alice said to her little sister. She cut her a piece the size of a fingernail. "It's not as bad as it looks—it's interesting."

Mary looked up trustingly at her sister, and then ate the piece. She chewed and chewed and chewed, seemingly forever, then finally swallowed.

"Okay, Alice, it wasn't so bad. Can I have some ice cream now?"

About the Author

Marie G. Lee, who is a Korean American, was born in Hibbing, Minnesota, in 1964. Her first published writing was an essay she submitted to *Seventeen* magazine when she was sixteen. She later worked in the field of economics and as an investment banker but is now a full-time writer. Lee's work has appeared in numerous newspapers and magazines. "A Taste of Korea" is an excerpt from her 1993 novel *If It Hadn't Been for Yoon Jun*.

Responding to the Story

▼ **Think Back**

What is Alice's relationship to the Larsens? What details give you clues about their family life?

What kind of people are the Lees? The Larsens?

How does Alice feel about the Lees?

▼ **Discuss**

Alice didn't know how to speak Korean, yet she felt that she "knew it" when she heard Yoon Jun and his mother talking. Have you ever had a similar feeling, either with a language or with music? Explain.

Yoon Jun makes noises while eating to show that he likes the food. In what other nonverbal ways do people show their liking for food?

What does Alice learn about eating a Korean meal? What other cultural differences does she observe?

▼ **Write**

Rewrite the Scene "A Taste of Korea" is written from the *third person point of view*. Although the narrator is outside the story, readers see the events from Alice's perspective. Rewrite the dinner scene from Yoon Jun's point of view.

Write a Short Story Write a story about dinner at a friend's house using third person point of view from your perspective. Then rewrite your story from your friend's perspective.

Hold the Sprouts

Dave Barry

Try the Sprout McBun!

What's the difference between fast food and slow food? Newspaper columnist Dave Barry knows, and he has a plan to make millions in the fast-food business.

I have figured out how to make several million dollars in the fast-food business.

First, let me give you a little background. As you know, in the past twenty years, fast-food restaurants have sprung up everywhere, like mildew; they have virtually replaced the old-fashioned slow-food restaurants, where you wasted valuable seconds selecting food from menus and waiting for it to be specially cooked and being served and eating with actual knives and forks from actual plates and so on. And why are the fast-food chains so successful? The answer is simple: *They serve only things that ten-year-olds like to eat.*

Fast-food-chain executives were the first to abandon the Balanced Diet Theory, which was popular with mothers when most of us were young. Remember? Your mother always fed you a balanced diet, which meant that for every food she served you that you could stand to eat, she served you another kind of food you could not stand to eat.

My mother stuck to this principle rigidly.[1] For example, if she served us something we sort of liked, such as beef stew, she also served us something we sort of disliked, such as green beans. And if she served us something we really liked, such as hamburgers, she made sure to also serve us something we really loathed, such as Brussels sprouts. We kids feared many things in those days—werewolves, dentists, North Koreans, Sunday school—but they all paled by comparison with Brussels sprouts. I can remember many a summer evening when I had eaten my hamburger in thirty-one seconds and was itching to go outside and commit acts of minor vandalism with my friends, but I had to sit at the table, staring for hours at Brussels sprouts congealing[2] on my plate, knowing that my mother would not let me leave until I had eaten them. In the end, I always ate them, because I knew she would let me starve to death before she would let me get out of eating my Brussels sprouts. That's how fervently[3] she believed in the Balanced Diet Theory. And, in those days, so did restaurants. When we went out to eat, we kids always ordered hamburgers and French fries, but they always were accompanied by some alien substance, such as peas.

But the old-fashioned, slow-food restaurant owners were fools to believe in the Balanced Diet Theory, because it does not take into account what people, particularly kids, really want to eat. Kids don't want to eat wholesome foods: kids want to eat grease and sugar. This is why, given the choice, kids will eat things that do not qualify as food at all, such as Cheez

[1] not ever changing

[2] thickening; becoming like jelly

[3] strongly; intensely

Doodles, Yoo-Hoo, Good 'n' Plenty and those little wax bottles that contain colored syrup with enough sugar per bottle to dissolve a bulldozer in two hours. As kids grow up, they reluctantly accept the idea that their diets should be balanced, and by the time they are thirty-five or forty years old they will eat peas voluntarily. But all of us, deep in our hearts, still want grease and sugar. That is what separates us from animals.

And that is why fast-food restaurants are so successful. At fast-food restaurants, you never run the risk of finding peas on your plate. You don't even get a plate. What you get is hamburgers and French fries; these are your primary sources of grease. You get your sugar from soft drinks or "shakes," which are milk shakes from which the milk has been eliminated on the grounds that milk has been identified by the United States Government as a major cause of nutrition.

At first, fast-food restaurants were popular only with wild teenaged hot rodders who carried switchblade knives and refused to eat Brussels sprouts. But then the fast-food chains realized they could make much more money if they could broaden their appeal, so they started running television ads to convince people, particularly mothers, that fast food is *wholesome*. You see these ads all the time: you have your wholesome Mom and your wholesome Dad and their 2.2 wholesome kids, and they're at the fast-food restaurant, just wolfing down grease and sugar, and they're having such a wholesome time that every now and then everybody in the whole place, including the counterpersons with the Star Trek uniforms, jumps up and sings and dances out of sheer joy. The message is clear: you can *forget* about the old Balanced Diet Theory; it's *okay* to eat this stuff.

Lately, the advertisements have started stressing how much *variety* you can get at fast-food restaurants. Besides hamburger, you can get chicken in a hamburger bun, roast beef in a hamburger bun, steak in a hamburger bun, and fish in a hamburger bun; you can even get an entire three-part breakfast in a hamburger bun. A fast-food restaurant near me recently started serving—I swear this is true—*veal parmigiana* in a hamburger bun. And people are *buying* it.

Besides hamburger, you can get chicken in a hamburger bun, roast beef in a hamburger bun, steak in a hamburger bun, and fish in a hamburger bun; you can even get an entire three-part breakfast in a hamburger bun.

This leads me to my plan to make several million dollars. My plan rests on two assumptions:[4]

- People have become so committed[5] to fast food that they don't care *what* they eat, as long as it's in a hamburger bun, and

[4] beliefs held without proof

[5] devoted; firmly pledged

- There must be an enormous world glut[6] of green vegetables, since nobody believes in the Balanced Diet Theory any more.

So I plan to buy several tons of Brussels sprouts, which I figure would cost a total of six dollars. I'll put them in hamburger buns, then get some actor to dress up as a clown or some other idiot character and go on television and urge everybody to rush right over and pay me $1.69 for a Sprout McBun. Before long, kids will be *begging* their parents to buy my Brussels sprouts, and I will be rich. I'll bet you wish you had thought of it.

About the Author

Dave Barry was born in 1947 in Armonk, New York. He is a Pulitzer-prize winning syndicated columnist for *The Miami Herald*. There are numerous collections of Barry's essays in print, including a travel guide to Japan. "Hold the Sprouts" is taken from his book *Bad Habits*.

Responding to the Essay

▼ Think Back

According to Dave Barry, why are fast-food restaurants so successful?

What is Barry's opinion of fast-food restaurants?

What is Barry's plan to make several million dollars?

▼ Discuss

If you had a choice of either eating at a fast-food restaurant or an old-fashioned, slow-food restaurant, which would you choose? Explain your answer.

In your opinion, how important is a balanced diet? How balanced is your diet?

▼ Write

Use Hyperbole *Hyperbole* is an extravagant exaggeration used to make a point. Dave Barry uses hyperbole to add humor to "Hold the Sprouts." For example, do you think that the little wax bottles that kids love contain enough colored syrup to dissolve a bulldozer in two hours? Use hyperbole to describe some unhealthy foods you eat.

Write a Restaurant Review Do you have a favorite "greasy spoon" restaurant, a place which might not serve the healthiest food, but a place that you like for its atmosphere? Write a review explaining why it is the best restaurant in town. Use hyperbole to add humor.

Stranger at the Table

Bob Greene

How would you feel if you found a stranger in your home? Columnist Bob Greene relates this true story of an uninvited guest.

It's hard to make any sense of this story; but then, it's becoming increasingly hard to make any sense of these times.

On a recent Saturday night a man named David Gambill was returning to his home in Richmond, Virginia. Gambill and his wife, Ayer, had been on a week's vacation to Massachusetts; now they were tired, and were anxious to get back to their own house.

They pulled into the driveway. Gambill opened the back door. It struck him right away that something was amiss.

There was food on the stove, and the food was cooking. Chow mein and six fish sticks. But there was no one in the kitchen.

Gambill told his wife to wait by the back door. He began to walk around his house. In a bathroom, he found that a window had been broken. Now he was sure that someone was in his house.

He went from room to room. Later his friends would tell him that he was crazy to do that; the friends would say that he should have gotten out of the house and called the police. But Gambill was determined to find out who was in his home.

He went into his son's bedroom. The door to his son's closet was closed. Gambill opened the door.

Sitting in the closet, huddled behind Gambill's son's rolled-up sleeping bag, was a bedraggled-looking old fellow.

"He looked awful," Gambill said. "He needed a shave, and he was wearing what I can only describe as thrift-shop clothing. The thing I remember most clearly was his eyes. They were just staring back at me. I knew right away that I wasn't in any danger. In his eyes I saw fear—fear and relief that I wasn't going to hurt him."

Gambill stood there staring at the man. The man started to speak.

"I was hungry," the man said. "I was hungry, so I came on into your house."

Gambill didn't know what to say to the man.

"You can call the police if you want," the man said.

Gambill thought of what he should do: pounce on the man, tie him up, lock him in the closet.

But he realized that what he was feeling wasn't anger. It was sadness.

"You really broke in because you were hungry?" Gambill said.

"Yes," the man said.

Gambill knew that, in looking around the house, nothing had been stolen. The only things that had been disturbed, with the exception of the broken bathroom window, were the chow mein and the fish sticks that had been taken from the Gambills' refrigerator and put on the stove.

"You can go in and finish your supper," Gambill said.

So the man straightened up, walked out of the closet, and went to the kitchen. As Gambill and his wife watched, the man put the chow mein and the fish sticks onto a plate, and sat down at the kitchen table.

Gambill, almost as a second thought, picked up the telephone and called the Henrico County police. He told the dispatcher[1] what had happened; the dispatcher said police officers would be over immediately.

"I couldn't believe how fast he ate that food," Gambill said. "He just kept putting it into his mouth as fast as he could.

"I know I probably shouldn't have let him do it. But when I thought about it—he was risking getting arrested so he could have a meal. He was risking his life, really. He could have got shot breaking into someone's house. If he was that desperate, I couldn't deny him the food."

The man finished his meal. He went over and got a water tumbler from the Gambills' shelf. He drew a glass of water from the kitchen sink. He gulped it down.

Gambill said he still felt no danger, being in the house with the man who had broken in. "He wasn't

[1] person who takes calls and responds or sends help

going to spring at me or anything," Gambill said. "There was no threat to me. He was very docile."[2]

[2] easy to manage

The police arrived. They entered the Gambills' kitchen, and Gambill immediately filled them in on what had happened. The police stared at the man, who was still in the kitchen, with the now-empty plate and glass. The man made no effort to flee.

The police began to read the man his Miranda rights.

"It was the most bizarre[3] scene," Gambill said. "The old guy was standing there, and the police were reading his rights to him, and it was like something off a television show. I kept staring at the old guy, and I kept hearing these phrases the police were reading: 'right to remain silent,' and 'right to an attorney.' The guy was showing no visible reaction."

[3] very unusual; weird

The police put the man in handcuffs and led him out to the squad car. As the man left, he said nothing to Gambill or his wife. Later, the police would charge the man—whom they identified as Allen Young, age approximately fifty-seven—with breaking and entering, and petty larceny.[4]

[4] theft of personal property

"I've felt terrible ever since that night," Gambill said. "I make a pretty good living; hunger isn't a big issue for me. We read about hunger, and we know it's out there, but it takes something like this to bring it home."

Gambill said that, in the days following the incident, he has gone through all the emotions that people who are burglarized often feel: a sense of violation, a sense of being helpless against outside forces, a sense of his home not being entirely his own any longer.

But the dominant[5] emotion was a different one.

"I don't know how to put this, but I almost felt like crying," he said. "Crying at the thought of what's going on out there for people like that fellow. Can you understand what I'm saying? I haven't been sleeping very well at night."

About the Author

Bob Greene was born in 1947 in Columbus, Ohio. His syndicated column appears in more than 200 newspapers. His published works include many collections of his columns; *Hang Time* and *Rebound*, biographies of Michael Jordan; and *Good Morning, Merry Sunshine*, a journal of the first year of his daughter's life. "Stranger at the Table" is reprinted from *Cheeseburgers: The Best of Bob Greene*.

Responding to the Essay

▼ Think Back

How did David Gambill know something was wrong when he and his wife returned home from vacation?

What feelings did Gambill have as he searched for, found, and fed Allen Young?

How did this experience change Gambill?

▼ Discuss

Did David Gambill do the right thing by calling the police? What would you have done in his situation?

If someone asked you for money to buy food, what would you do? How might you feel?

What conclusions can you draw about our society from David Gambill's experience?

▼ Write

Add Quotations Bob Greene includes quotations from Gambill that describe his thoughts and emotions. Are there other parts of the essay that you think could use quotations? Write what you think one of the participants might have said.

Write a Description Think about an exciting event in which you were a participant. Write a description of it. Interview other participants to get their thoughts and feelings. Include their words in quotations.

Theme Links
Food for Thought

At first glance someone might think that the selections you have just read were about food. In reality, you read about the broader issues of cultural diversity, childhood memories, and homelessness. How do the diverse topics of these thought-provoking selections relate to you?

▼ Group Discussion

With a partner or in a small group, talk about the selections in this unit and how they relate to the theme and to your own lives. Use questions like the following to guide the discussion.

- What did the writers or characters reveal about themselves, their generations, or their cultures through their discussions about food?
- Why do certain foods spark vivid memories?
- If you were to write an essay for this unit, what would it be about? What food or situation would you use to introduce your topic?

▼ An Interview with Allen Young

Bob Greene's essay "Stranger at the Table" described how desperate a hungry man became. With a partner, role-play an interview between Allen Young, the homeless man who broke into David Gambill's house, and an investigative reporter. Write questions and responses, and then conduct the interview for the class.

▼ Food Chart

How does the food of a country reflect its geography, climate, and culture? With a group, choose three countries and make a chart illustrating typical foods, the geography, the climate, and interesting features of the culture for each country. Share the chart with the class. Can you see relationships between the categories? For example, the fact that fish is an important part of a Japanese diet is related to the fact that Japan is a country of islands.

▼ Mouth-Watering Memory

What food brings fond memories to your mind? Either copy a recipe or write a detailed description of that food. Then explain why the memory is so special.

▼ The Theme and You

Write an action plan that details ways in which to feed the homeless. Describe the foods needed, where and how you would collect the food, the best ways to distribute it, and ways to generate more interest and concern among your fellow classmates and citizens.

American History

While reading a good story or an interesting essay, you might also learn something about history. Authors often weave historical facts into their works. The plot of a story or the attitudes of a writer can be affected by a historical setting or by historical events at the time a piece is written.

Through the personal accounts and historical fiction in this unit, you will share the experiences of a newly freed slave and a Lakota Sioux boy on a buffalo hunt. You will learn the thoughts and feelings of soldiers at war and of someone who is discriminated against because of her race.

As you read these selections, try to visualize the characters. Which of them would you like to meet? What questions would you like to ask them?

Letters from the Front

The Civil War began in April of 1861. In July, a week before the Battle of Bull Run, Major Sullivan Ballou of the 2nd Rhode Island wrote a letter to his wife in Smithfield. What are some things he wants her to know?

[1] forced; strongly moved

July 14, 1861
Camp Clark, Washington

My very dear Sarah:

The indications are very strong that we shall move in a few days—perhaps tomorrow. Lest I should not be able to write again, I feel impelled[1] to write a few lines that may fall under your eye when I shall be no more. . . .

I have no misgivings about, or lack of confidence in the cause in which I am engaged, and my courage does not halt or falter. I know how strongly American Civilization now leans on the triumph of the Government, and how great a debt we owe to those who went before us through the blood and sufferings of the Revolution. And I am willing—perfectly willing—to lay down all my joys in this life, to help maintain this Government, and to pay that debt. . . .

Sarah my love for you is deathless, it seems to bind me with mighty cables that nothing but

Omnipotence[2] could break; and yet my love of Country comes over me like a strong wind and bears me unresistibly on with all these chains to the battle field.

[2] God

The memories of the blissful[3] moments I have spent with you come creeping over me, and I feel most gratified to God and to you that I have enjoyed them so long. And hard it is for me to give them up and burn to ashes the hopes of future years, when, God willing, we might still have lived and loved together, and seen our sons grown up to honorable manhood, around us.
I have, I know, but few and small claims upon Divine Providence, but something whispers to me—perhaps it is the wafted[4] prayer of my little Edgar, that I shall return to my loved ones unharmed. If I do not my dear Sarah, never forget how much I love you, and when my last breath escapes me on the battle field, it will whisper your name. Forgive my many faults, and the many pains I have caused you. How thoughtless and foolish I have often times been! How gladly would I wash out with my tears every little spot upon your happiness. . . .

[3] happy

[4] carried along; transported

But, O Sarah! if the dead can come back to this earth and flit unseen around those they loved, I shall always be near you; in the gladdest days and in the darkest nights . . . *always, always,* and if there be a soft breeze upon your cheek, it shall be my breath, as the cool air fans your throbbing temple, it shall be my spirit passing by. Sarah do not mourn me dead; think I am gone and wait for thee, for we shall meet again. . . .

Major Sullivan Ballou was killed at the first battle of Bull Run [on July 21, 1861].

This letter was written to family members in Ohio by a nurse serving in Vietnam. She includes details of the long days spent in a jungle climate. How do her words let you share her experiences?

United States troops were heavily involved in the Vietnam War from 1965 to 1973. As the war dragged on, Americans were debating their country's involvement. Many people wanted peace at home and our troops out of Vietnam.

4 June 1969
Wednesday

Dear Mom & Dad,

Got your letter of 28th, Mom, yesterday, 3 June. Today I got Dad's of 26th April. Never know what is going on with the mail. Haven't gotten the package yet. Heaven only knows when they will arrive and in what condition.

Worked in ICU [Intensive Care Unit] again today. Was lucky, got to 102° today, and ICU is air-conditioned. They have a lot of really sick patients. Had three die yesterday. They still have four on respirators.[1] None too good, either.

One of the GI's who died yesterday was from Ward 8, medical. Had malaria.[2] During the previous night he had been nauseated and kept getting up to the latrine[3] to vomit. Got up at 2 A.M. and was running to the latrine. Fell really hard and cracked his head on the cement floor. The nurse who was on duty said you could *hear* his skull fracture. He immediately started bleeding from ears and nose and stopped breathing. Then had cardiac arrest.[4] They got him going again and transferred him to ICU but he died anyway yesterday.

[1] machines to help people breathe

[2] a disease caused by the bite of an infected mosquito

[3] bathroom

[4] failure of the heart to pump blood

Had severe brain damage. Other death was [a] GI with multiple fragment wounds from a mine explosion. He was there two weeks ago when I worked that other day in ICU. Also a Vietnamese died. Don't know what was wrong with him.

Census hit the 10,000 mark yesterday. This unit, the 312th [Evacuation Hospital], has treated 10,000 patients since [we] arrived last September. Unbelievable. Registrar office had a poll going as to what time and what date the 10,000th patient would be admitted. Was yesterday morning. Haven't heard who won the money yet.

They put plastic or rubber? floor tile down in the mess hall the evening before last. Looked real nice until yesterday noon when it got hot. The tar came up between the tile and it got tracked all over the place. Couldn't move your chair at all. It was stuck to the floor.

How did the home-made ice cream turn out? Start "nights" tomorrow so don't have to get up early tomorrow. Nice thought.

Still very quiet around here. Haven't gotten mortared[5] for couple of weeks now. We are getting some new nurses this week. They are from the unit who will take over when the 312th goes home in September. Their hospital is farther south somewhere. They are handling 80% Vietnamese casualties now so are turning their hospital over to the Viets and coming here to take over. Supposed to get the new chief nurse tomorrow. So

[5] shelled; fired on by cannons

the unit will change names in September. However, they were supposed to be an RA [Regular Army] group. Not a reserve unit like the 312th is. Things are supposed to get a lot more "strict Army style." No one is looking forward to it.

Read a book last night and missed a good Lee Marvin movie at the mess hall.

Had a movie star visit here the second or third week I was here. Named Ricardo Montalban? Ever hear of him? Forgot to mention it previously. Some of the older people here remembered him. Said he was in movies with Esther Williams.

Will stop for now. Getting sleepy.

See you sooner.

Shar

1Lt. Sharon A. Lane, a nurse from Canton, Ohio, arrived at the 312th Evacuation Hospital, Chu Lai, in April 1969. Two months later, on 8 June, she was killed by shrapnel during a rocket attack. She was one month short of her 26th birthday.

Responding to the Letters

▼ Think Back

What promise does Sullivan Ballou make to his wife?

What is Sharon Lane's attitude toward her work? What details give you clues about how she feels?

How does Ballou's letter differ from Lane's?

▼ Discuss

How is writing a letter to someone different from talking in person? What can you say in a letter that you might not say in person? Why?

Besides facing danger, soldiers who go to war miss the people and things that are familiar to them. How would you feel about going to war? What would you miss?

▼ Write

Notice the Style These letters reflect the authors' natural writing styles as well as the styles of the historical periods. Sullivan Ballou writes in a formal, sentimental style. Sharon Lane writes informally in a conversational style. Try reversing the styles. Rewrite Ballou's letter in a conversational style or Lane's in a formal style.

Write a Letter Imagine that you are separated from someone you care about. Write a letter to that person describing your thoughts and feelings. Then examine your letter. What is your natural writing style? What makes your style unique and personal?

When Freedom Came

Julius Lester

The Civil War is over and Jake is set free. He and his family had been owned by a Southern slaveholder. Several years before the war ended, Jake's wife and children were sold to someone else and taken away. Now Jake is free and sets out to find them.

The Civil War ended in 1865, and the slaves were set free. Freedom was sweet, but life was still hard, and not everyone lived "happily ever after." What problems do you think newly freed slaves might face?

Pulaski, Tennessee, was more than five hundred miles from Pine Bluff, Arkansas. Jake wished he was a bird and could have flown those miles in a couple of days. But he had to walk them, one step at a time, one foot in front of the other. And he couldn't walk every day, because he had to stop and work to get at least enough to eat. Sometimes he got paid in money, and for a few days he could travel and buy enough to eat.

There were a lot of ex-slaves traveling the roads. Some were also looking for children, wives, husbands, or parents who had been sold. It helped him to know that he wasn't the only one. Some he talked to hadn't seen their mothers since they were children. He knew how they felt. It helped a man to know where he was from if he knew where his mother was. His mother lay in the slave burying ground on the plantation.[1]

He wondered sometimes how many people looking for loved ones would find them, including himself. In a way it was a foolish thing to do. But there was no way not to do it. Every day someone asked him if he knew such-and-such a person or if he had heard anything about them. After three months on the road he found that he had a vast store of information and several times was able to direct someone a little closer to the person he was looking for. And just as he was asked, he asked. But it wasn't until he had passed through Nashville, Tennessee, did he find someone who thought she knew Mandy. It was an old woman, who reminded him of Aunt Kate, walking down the road with a bundle on her head. Like many others, she didn't know where she was going but, "Where ain't as important as the going, son," she said, laughing. "You know when you let a chicken out of a coop, it don't have the slightest idea where it's going. Might run out in the woods and get eaten by a fox first thing. But all the chickens know is to get away from the coop."

He asked her about Mandy and gave a description of her.

The old lady nodded. "She got some children?"

Jake nodded.

"And she dark skin, you say? Like you is?"

"That's right," he said, getting excited.

[1] a large farm or estate where the crops are cared for by workers who live there

"Well, if it's the same Mandy, she live on Mr. Jim Jenkenson's place on the other side of Pulaski. When you gets in the vicinity,[2] son, you just ask somebody to direct you to Mr. Jim Jenkenson's place. Everybody 'round there know where it is. If it's the same Mandy, she be out there."

"How many days walking is that?"

"Three days if you stroll. Two and a half if you walk fast. And a day if you can hitch a ride on somebody's mule cart."

Jake tried not to let himself get too excited. It might be another Mandy. It was a common name. But the old woman said it was outside of Pulaski and that was where Mandy had been sold, too. Still, he kept his feelings inside of him, as if they were a present tied up in a red ribbon which he could open only on Christmas.

It took him two days of fast walking with little sleep to get to Pulaski, and the first person he asked directed him to continue down the road for another two miles. He asked that person if he knew Mandy, and the person nodded and said Mandy had six children. Jake was disappointed. Mandy only had four. He almost didn't go any farther, but since he was so close, he decided to go on. Maybe the person had made a mistake about the number of children she had.

She was walking down the road carrying a bucket of water on her head when he saw her. He knew it was she, the one arm raised over her head, resting lightly against the bucket, the other arm swinging loosely at her side. He had always loved the easy way Mandy had of walking, even with a bucket of water on her head. She never looked like she was working. He started to call out her name, but stopped. It was just possible that it was somebody else. Sometimes every woman he saw looked like Mandy, so he started running to catch up with her.

The woman heard the hurried steps behind her and stopped to look back. Jake saw the soft black face he had loved all of his life and shouted, "It's you! It's you! Mandy!" He ran up to her, tears running down his face. "Oh, thank God. Mandy!"

"Jake? Is that you, Jake?"

"It ain't Abraham Lincoln," he said, laughing.

She gazed at him, uncertain what to do. Then, letting her hand drop from the bucket she screamed, "Jake!" as the bucket tumbled from her head and water splashed both of them. She flung her arms around him, laughing. "Jake, Jake, Jake. It is you, ain't it?"

***

Jake saw the soft black face he had loved all of his life and shouted, "It's you! It's you! Mandy!"

***

And with the feel of her arms pressing against his back, Jake felt himself come to life for the first time since he'd last seen her. He buried his face in her neck.

"I told you that if anything ever happened, I'd find you. I told you, didn't I?"

"You look just the same," Mandy said, looking at him. "Just the same." She stepped out of his arms and picked up the bucket, laughing. "Look what you made me do. Now I got to go all the way back to the spring and get some more."

"Well, come on. How's Charles and Mary Ann and Caesar and Carl?" he asked, referring to the children.

"Oh, they fine. You probably won't recognize none of 'em. They so big now."

He laughed. "And to think that I almost didn't come out here."

"What you mean?"

"Well, I asked after you in town and a man said he knew of a Mandy who had six children and since we only got four, I just figured it was another Mandy. I almost didn't come, till it occurred to me that he might have made a mistake."

They came to the spring and Mandy bent to fill the bucket.

"Let me do it," Jake said. "You ain't gon' be toting no more water now. And anyway, how come Charles or one of the other children didn't come and get it?"

"They out in the field."

"Well, from now on you ain't gon' be doing no more of that heavy lifting and work like that." Jake filled the bucket. "I never could carry it on my head like you."

"Jake? Set that bucket down." She laughed, looking at him trying to set it on his head.

"I'll carry it," Jake said proudly.

"Set it down," she said, suddenly sad.

He put it on the ground and looked at her. "Anything the matter?"

She nodded. "I ain't your wife no more, Jake," she said sadly, looking at her feet. "That man in town what told you I got six children now was telling the truth. I should've told you back on the road when you brought it up. But I didn't know how to tell you."

"You ain't married to somebody else?"

She nodded and broke into tears. "How was I to know for sure you'd find me, Jake? I could've waited for you until the day I died and you never showed up 'cause you was dead or had done married somebody else."

"Aw, Mandy," he cried, taking her in his arms. "But I told you I'd find you, didn't I? I told you that!"

"I know, Jake, and I wanted to believe you. God knows I did. But a woman gets lonesome, Jake. And Henry was a nice man. The children liked him, too. So we jumped the broom³ and I prayed that this time the Lord wouldn't let me or him be sold away from each other. And after we was freed, the first thing we done was to go and get married like white folks do, and get a piece of paper so couldn't nobody come and separate us. If I'd known, Jake, I wouldn't have done it. But a woman gets lonesome."

"So do a man," he sobbed. "So do a man."

They held each other tightly for a while. "I just wish I'd known, Jake," she whispered softly, stepping back and wiping her eyes.

³ got married in a ceremony practiced by African American slaves

"Mandy? You ain't got to stay, do you?" Jake said, getting excited. "Now that I'm here, you can leave and come with me."

Mandy shook her head. "I can't do that, Jake. I swore before God and the preacher to be with Henry until one of us died. And, plus, we got married by the paper, the way the white folks do. And when you get the paper, you married sho' 'nuf. It ain't like jumping the broom. Like we done in slavery time. We ain't slaves no more, Jake. We got to live by the paper now."

"But, Mandy, I love you! I ain't thought about nothing else for seven years but you!"

She started crying again. "I loves you, too, Jake. God knows I do. But Henry's a good man, and I don't love him like I do you, but I guess I love him. I loved him enough to get married by the paper."

Jake shook his head repeatedly, muttering, "No, no, no, no. It ain't right. First they come and take you away, sell you like you a bale of cotton. They don't ask me how my heart feels about it. Just sell you away. Then you meets somebody you don't love like you love me, but they give you a piece of paper saying you got to be with him, though you love me. It ain't right, Mandy. It just ain't right."

"But that's the way it is, Jake. Wasn't right for us to be slaves all them years neither, but that was the way it was." She picked up the bucket of water and hoisted it to her head. "I—I got to be getting back, Jake. You want to come see the children? I know Henry wouldn't mind. I told him all about you and he say you sound like a very good man, the kind of man he'd like to know. I know you'd like him too Jake. Ain't none of this his fault."

"I know that, Mandy. But I reckon not. I don't think I could stand seeing another man happy with you."

She nodded. "I understands."

She started up the path from the spring to the road. Jake didn't move. He raised his head and watched the easy swaying of her body. When she got to the road she turned and looked at him. He could see the tears coming down her face.

"I wish I'd known, Jake."

"God knows, I wished you had too, Mandy," he said, biting his lip and sobbing as he watched her walk down the road and out of sight.

About the Author

Julius Lester was born in 1939 in St. Louis, Missouri. He has written numerous essays and reviews and is a collector and writer of African American folklore and stories from black history. This story is an excerpt from his book *Long Journey Home: Stories from Black History*. That book and his *To Be A Slave* showcase ordinary people in adverse circumstances and, as Lester says, provide the reader with a look at "history from the bottom up."

Responding to the Story

▼ Think Back

What obstacles did Jake overcome to reach Tennessee?

How did Jake and other ex-slaves find lost loved ones?

How did Jake and Mandy react when they realized that they would not be together again?

▼ Discuss

Does Mandy do the right thing by staying loyal to Henry, even though she doesn't love him as she loves Jake?

Is this a love story, or a story about slavery? Could it be both? How did the author weave a history lesson into the story of Mandy and Jake?

▼ Write

Write a Character Sketch Skim "When Freedom Came" and pick out examples of dialogue that reveal what the characters are like. Using the dialogue as support, write a personality sketch of one of the characters.

Continue the Story Try your hand at writing dialogue by picking up Jake's story where Julius Lester left off. Think about the following questions:

- What will Jake do next?
- Who will he meet or talk to?
- Where will he go? Will he go back to see Mandy and his children?

At Last I Kill a Buffalo

Chief Luther Standing Bear

 At last the day came when my father allowed me to go on a buffalo hunt with him. And what a proud boy I was!

Ever since I could remember, my father had been teaching me the things that I should know and preparing me to be a good hunter. I had learned to make bows and to string them; and to make arrows and tip them with feathers. I knew how to ride my pony no matter how fast he would go, and I felt that I was brave and did not fear danger. All these things I had learned for just this day when father would allow me to go with him on a buffalo hunt. It was the event for which every Sioux boy eagerly waited. To ride side by side with the best hunters of the tribe, to hear the terrible noise of the great herds as they ran, and then to help to bring home the kill was the most thrilling day of any Indian boy's life. The only other event which could equal it would be the day I went for the first time on the warpath to meet the enemy and protect my tribe.

Luther Standing Bear, a member of the Lakota Sioux group of Native Americans, grew up in the 1800s. It was an honor for a Sioux boy to go with adults on a buffalo hunt. How does his first hunt test Standing Bear's character?

On the following early morning we were to start, so the evening was spent in preparation. Although the tipis were full of activity, there was no noise nor confusion outside. Always the evening before a buffalo hunt and when every one was usually in his tipi, an old man went around the circle of tipis calling, 'I-ni-la,' 'I-ni-la,' not loudly, but so every one could hear. The old man was saying, 'Keep quiet,' 'Keep quiet.' We all knew that the scouts had come in and reported buffalo near and that we must all keep the camp in stillness. It was not necessary for the old man to go into each tipi and explain to the men that tomorrow there would be a big hunt, as the buffalo were coming. He did not order the men to prepare their weapons and neither did he order the mothers to keep children from crying. The one word, 'I-ni-la,' was sufficient[1] to bring quiet to the whole camp. That night there would be no calling or shouting from tipi to tipi and no child would cry aloud. Even the horses and dogs obeyed the command for quiet, and all night not a horse neighed and not a dog barked. The very presence of quiet was everywhere. Such is the orderliness of a Sioux camp that men, women, children, and animals seem to have a common understanding and sympathy. It is no mystery but natural that the Indian and his animals understand each other very well both with words and without words. There are words, however, that the Indian uses that are understood by both his horses and dogs. When on a hunt, if one of the warriors speaks a word 'A-a-ah' rather quickly and sharply, every man, horse, and dog will stop

[1] enough

instantly and listen. Not a move will be made by an animal until the men move or speak further. As long as the hunters listen, the animals will listen also.

The night preceding a buffalo hunt was always an exciting night, even though it was quiet in camp. There would be much talk in the tipis around the fires. There would be sharpening of arrows and of knives. New bow-strings would be made and quivers would be filled with arrows.

It was in the fall of the year and the evenings were cool as father and I sat by the fire and talked over the hunt. I was only eight years of age, and I know that father did not expect me to get a buffalo at all, but only to try perhaps for a small calf should I be able to get close enough to one. Nevertheless, I was greatly excited as I sat and watched father working in his easy, firm way.

I was wearing my buffalo-skin robe, the hair next to my body. Mother had made me a rawhide belt and this, wrapped around my waist, held my blanket on when I threw it off my shoulders. In the early morning I would wear it, for it would be cold. When it came time to shoot, I should not want my blanket but the belt would hold it in place.

You can picture me, I think, as I sat in the glow of the camp-fire, my little brown body bare to the waist watching, and listening intently to my father. My hair hung down my back and I wore moccasins and breech-cloth of buckskin. To my belt was fastened a rawhide holster for my knife, for when I was eight years of age we had plenty of knives. I was proud to own a knife, and this night I remember I kept it on all night. Neither did I lay aside my bow, but went to sleep with it in my hand, thinking, I suppose, to be all the nearer ready in the morning when the start was made.

Father sharpened my steel points for me and also sharpened my knife. The whetstone was a long stone which was kept in a buckskin bag, and sometimes this stone went all over the camp; every tipi did not have one, so we shared this commodity[2] with one another. I had as I remember about ten arrows, so when father was through sharpening them I put them in my rawhide quiver. I had a rawhide quirt,[3] too, which I would wear fastened to my waist. As father worked, he knew I was watching him closely and listening whenever he spoke. By the time all preparations had been made, he told me just how I was to act when I started out in the morning with the hunters.

We went to bed, my father hoping that tomorrow would be successful for him so that he could bring home some nice meat for the family and a hide for my mother to tan. I went to bed, but could not go to sleep at once, so filled was I with the wonderment and excitement of it all. The next day was to be a test for me. I was to prove to my father whether he was or was not justified in his pride in me. What would be the result of my training? Would I be brave if I faced danger and would father be proud of me? Though I did not know it that night I was to be tried for the strength of my manhood and my honesty in this hunt. Something happened that day which I remember above all things. It was a test of

[2] a useful thing

[3] a riding whip with a short handle

my real character and I am proud to say that I did not find myself weak, but made a decision that has been all these years a gratification[4] to me.

[4] cause for being pleased with oneself

The next morning the hunters were catching their horses about daybreak. I arose with my father and went out and caught my pony. I wanted to do whatever he did and show him that he did not have to tell me what to do. We brought our animals to the tipi and got our bows and arrows and mounted. From over the village came the hunters. Most of them were leading their running horses. These running horses were anxious for the hunt and came prancing, their ears straight up and their tails waving in the air. We were joined with perhaps a hundred or more riders, some of whom carried bows and arrows and some armed with guns.

I arose with my father and went out and caught my pony. I wanted to do whatever he did and show him that he did not have to tell me what to do.

The buffalo were reported to be about five or six miles away as we should count distance now. At that time we did not measure distance in miles. One camping distance was about ten miles, and these buffalo were said to be about one half camping distance away.

Some of the horses were to be left at a stopping place just before the herd was reached. These horses were pack animals which were taken along to carry extra blankets or weapons. They were trained to remain there until the hunters came for them. Though they were neither hobbled[5] nor tied, they stood still during the shooting and noise of the chase.

My pony was a black one and a good runner. I felt very important as I rode along with the hunters and my father, the chief. I kept as close to him as I could.

Two men had been chosen to scout or to lead the party. These two men were in a sense policemen whose work it was to keep order. They carried large sticks of ash wood, something like a policeman's billy, though longer. They rode ahead of the party while the rest of us kept in a group close together. The leaders went ahead until they sighted the herd of grazing buffalo. Then they stopped and waited for the rest of us to ride up. We all rode slowly toward the herd, which on sight of us had come together, although they had been scattered here and there over the plain. When they saw us, they all ran close together as if at the command of a leader. We continued riding slowly toward the herd until one of the leaders shouted, 'Ho-ka-he!' which means, 'Ready, Go!' At that command every man started for the herd. I had been listening, too, and the minute the hunters started, I started also.

Away I went, my little pony putting all he had into the race. It was not long before I lost sight of father, but I kept going just the same. I threw my

[5] having the legs fastened together to prevent straying

blanket back and the chill of the autumn morning struck my body, but I did not mind. On I went. It was wonderful to race over the ground with all these horsemen about me. There was no shouting, no noise of any kind except the pounding of the horses' feet. The herd was now running and had raised a cloud of dust. I felt no fear until we had entered this cloud of dust and I could see nothing about me—only hear the sound of feet. Where was father? Where was I going? On I rode through the cloud, for I knew I must keep going.

On I went. It was wonderful to race over the ground with all these horsemen about me. There was no shouting, no noise of any kind except the pounding of the horses' feet.

Then all at once I realized that I was in the midst of the buffalo, their dark bodies rushing all about me and their great heads moving up and down to the sound of their hoofs beating upon the earth. Then it was that fear overcame me and I leaned close down upon my little pony's body and clutched him tightly. I can never tell you how I felt toward my pony at that moment. All thought of shooting had left my mind. I was seized by blank fear. In a moment or so, however, my senses became clearer, and I could distinguish[6] other sounds beside the clatter of feet. I could hear a shot now and then and I could see the buffalo beginning to break up into small bunches. I could not see father nor any of my companions yet, but my fear was vanishing and I was safe. I let my pony run. The buffalo looked too large for me to tackle, anyway, so I just kept going. The buffalo became more and more scattered. Pretty soon I saw a young calf that looked about my size. I remembered now what father had told me the night before as we sat about the fire. Those instructions were important for me now to follow.

I was still back of the calf, being unable to get alongside of him. I was anxious to get a shot, yet afraid to try, as I was still very nervous. While my pony was making all speed to come alongside, I chanced a shot and to my surprise my arrow landed. My second arrow glanced along the back of the animal and sped on between the horns, making only a slight wound. My third arrow hit a spot that made the running beast slow up in his gait. I shot a fourth arrow, and though it, too, landed it was not a fatal wound. It seemed to me that it was taking a lot of shots, and I was not proud of my marksmanship. I was glad, however, to see the animal going slower and I knew that one more shot would make me a hunter. My horse seemed to know his own importance. His two ears stood straight forward and it was not necessary for me to urge him to get closer to the buffalo. I was soon by the side of the buffalo and one more shot brought the chase to a close. I jumped

from my pony, and as I stood by my fallen game, I
looked all around wishing that the world could see. But
I was alone. In my determination[7] to stay by until I had
won my buffalo, I had not noticed that I was far from
every one else. No admiring friends were about, and as
far as I could see I was on the plain alone. The herd of
buffalo had completely disappeared. And as for father,
much as I wished for him, he was out of sight and I had
no idea where he was.

**. . . I looked all around
wishing that the world could
see. But I was alone. In my
determination to stay by until
I had won my buffalo, I had
not noticed that I was far
from every one else.**

I stood and looked at the animal on the ground.
I was happy. Every one must know that I, Ota K'te, had
killed a buffalo. But it looked as if no one knew where I
was, so no one was coming my way. I must then take
something from this animal to show that I had killed it.
I took all the arrows one by one from the body. As I
took them out, it occurred to me that I had used five
arrows. If I had been a skillful hunter, one arrow would
have been sufficient, but I had used five. Here it was

that temptation came to me. Why could I not take out two of the arrows and throw them away? No one would know, and then I should be more greatly admired and praised as a hunter. As it was, I knew that I should be praised by father and mother, but I wanted more. And so I was tempted to lie.

I was planning this as I took out my skinning knife that father had sharpened for me the night before. I skinned one side of the animal, but when it came to turning it over, I was too small. I was wondering what to do when I heard my father's voice calling, 'To-ki-i-la-la-hu-wo,' 'Where are you?' I quickly jumped on my pony and rode to the top of a little hill near by. Father saw me and came to me at once. He was so pleased to see me and glad to know that I was safe. I knew that I could never lie to my father. He was too fond of me and I too proud of him. He had always told me to tell the truth. He wanted me to be an honest man, so I resolved then to tell the truth even if it took from me a little glory. He rode up to me with a glad expression on his face, expecting me to go back with him to his kill. As he came up, I said as calmly as I could, 'Father, I have killed a buffalo.' His smile changed to surprise and he asked me where my buffalo was. I pointed to it and we rode over to where it lay, partly skinned.

Father set to work to skin it for me. I had watched him do this many times and knew perfectly well how to do it myself, but I could not turn the animal over. There was a way to turn the head of the animal so that the body would be balanced on the back while being skinned. Father did this for me, while I helped all I could. When the hide was off, father put it on the pony's back with the hair side next to the pony. On this he arranged the meat so it would balance. Then he covered the meat carefully with the rest of the hide, so no dust would reach it while we traveled home. I rode home on top of the load.

I am more proud now that I told the truth than I am of killing the buffalo.

I showed my father the arrows that I had used and just where the animal had been hit. He was very pleased and praised me over and over again. I felt more glad than ever that I had told the truth and I have never regretted it. I am more proud now that I told the truth than I am of killing the buffalo.

We then rode to where my father had killed a buffalo. There we stopped and prepared it for taking home. It was late afternoon when we got back to camp. No king ever rode in state who was more proud than I that day as I came into the village sitting high up on my load of buffalo meat. Mother had now two hunters in the family and I knew how she was going to make over me. It is not customary for Indian men to brag about their exploits[8] and I had been taught that bragging was not nice. So I was very quiet, although I was bursting

[8] deeds; accomplishments

with pride. Always when arriving home I would run out to play, for I loved to be with the other boys, but this day I lingered about close to the tipi so I could hear the nice things that were said about me. It was soon all over camp that Ota K'te had killed a buffalo.

My father was so proud that he gave away a fine horse. He called an old man to our tipi to cry out the news to the rest of the people in camp. The old man stood at the door of our tipi and sang a song of praise to my father. The horse had been led up and I stood holding it by a rope. The old man who was doing the singing called the other old man who was to receive the horse as a present. He accepted the horse by coming up to me, holding out his hands to me, and saying, 'Ha-ye,' which means 'Thank you.' The old man went away very grateful for the horse.

That ended my first and last buffalo hunt. It lives only in my memory, for the days of the buffalo are over.

About the Author

Luther Standing Bear was born in the 1860s. In his memoir, *My Indian Boyhood*, he recounts his family life and upbringing within traditional Lakota society. When Luther Standing Bear was eight years old, he was allowed to take part in his first buffalo hunt. For him, as for all Lakota boys, it served as a test of his courage and ability.

Responding to the Autobiography

▼ Think Back

Why was a Sioux boy's first buffalo hunt special?

What was the relationship between the Sioux people and their animals?

What character traits did Luther Standing Bear and his Sioux peers value the most? How do you know?

▼ Discuss

Do you think that eight years of age is too young to participate in a dangerous task like a buffalo hunt? Why?

What do you learn about the Sioux way of life from this story of a first buffalo hunt? What do you learn about the relationship between the boy and his father?

▼ Write

Recognize Sequence Standing Bear describes the events of the buffalo hunt in chronological order, using transition words to show a change in time or sequence of events. Summarize his account by listing the events in chronological order.

Describe a Process Write a chronological account of the steps you use to prepare for an event. Use transition words to show sequence.

IN RESPONSE TO EXECUTIVE ORDER 9066

ALL AMERICANS OF JAPANESE DESCENT MUST REPORT TO RELOCATION CENTERS

Dwight Okita

How would you feel if your friends called you an enemy of your country? During World War II, Japanese citizens of the United States were forced to leave their homes and businesses. They were sent to special camps because some people believed they might be dangerous. This poem will help you understand one teenager's feelings.

Dear Sirs:

Of course I'll come. I've packed my galoshes
and three packets of tomato seeds. Denise calls them
love apples. My father says where we're going
they won't grow.

I am a fourteen-year-old girl with bad spelling
and a messy room. If it helps any, I will tell you
I have always felt funny using chopsticks
and my favorite food is hot dogs.
My best friend is a white girl named Denise—
we look at boys together. She sat in front of me
all through grade school because of our names:
O'Connor, Ozawa. I know the back of Denise's head
  very well.

I tell her she's going bald. She tells me I copy on tests.

We are best friends.

I saw Denise today in Geography class.

She was sitting on the other side of the room.

"You're trying to start a war," she said, "giving secrets

away to the Enemy, Why can't you keep your big

mouth shut?"

I didn't know what to say.

I gave her a packet of tomato seeds

and asked her to plant them for me, told her

when the first tomato ripened

she'd miss me.

About the Author

Dwight Okita, who was born in Illinois in 1958, is a playwright as well as a poet. "IN RESPONSE TO EXECUTIVE ORDER 9066" is from his first collection of poems, *Crossing with the Light*, which was published in 1982.

Responding to the Poem

▼ Think Back

How would you describe the speaker?

How do you know the speaker was upset with Denise?

How are the speaker and her best friend similar? How are they different?

▼ Discuss

Why do you think Dwight Okita wrote this poem in the form of a letter? Does the poem sound like a response to a government order or more like a response to a personal invitation? Explain your answer.

Why would Denise say such mean things to her best friend? What did she mean when she said the speaker was "giving secrets away to the Enemy"?

▼ Write

Write a Character Sketch You know what the speaker in this poem is like because she describes herself. She also tells us some things about her friend Denise. Based on this information, write a character sketch of Denise.

Rewrite the Poem Think about how the poem would be different if the speaker was different. What would a nine-year-old boy or an elderly woman say? Decide who your speaker will be. List some details that would be different. Then rewrite the poem from that person's perspective.

Around Brick Walls

S a r a h   D e l a n y

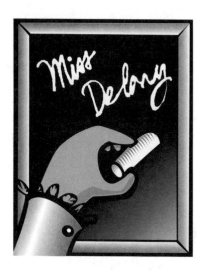

I had wanted to teach at a high school because it was considered a promotion, and it paid better. But I had to be a little clever—Bessie would say sneaky—to find ways to get around these brick walls they set up for colored folks. So I asked around quietly for some advice. A friend of my bother Hubert's who worked for the Board of Education suggested a plan, which I followed.

This is what I did: I applied for a high school position, and when I reached the top of the seniority[1] list after three years, I received a letter in the mail saying they wished to meet with me in person. At the appointment, they would have seen I was colored and found some excuse to bounce me down the list. So I skipped the appointment and sent them a letter, acting like there was a mix-up. Then I just showed up on the first day of classes. It was risky, but I knew what a bureaucracy[2] it was, and that in a bureaucracy it's easier to keep people out than to push them back down.

In this excerpt from *Having Our Say—The Delany Sisters' First 100 Years*, Sarah Delany tells how she broke new ground as the first black teacher in an all-white school. What gave her the courage to face such odds?

[1] number of years on the job

[2] complicated system of government

Child, when I showed up that day—at Theodore Roosevelt High School, a white high school—they just about died when they saw me. A colored woman! But my name was on the list to teach there, and it was too late for them to send me someplace else. The plan had worked! Once I was in, they couldn't figure out how to get rid of me.

So I became the first colored teacher in the New York City system to teach domestic science[3] on the high school level. I spent the rest of my career teaching at excellent high schools! Between 1930 and 1960, when I retired, I taught at Theodore Roosevelt High School, which is on Fordham Road in the Bronx, then at Girls' High School in Brooklyn, and finally at Evander Childs High School, which is on Gun Hill Road in the Bronx.

Plus, I got a night job—at Washington Irving High School in lower Manhattan—teaching adults who had dropped out of school. This was something I really wanted to do. The way I got the job was that the girl who had it before me complained a lot, was late a lot, and would ask me to substitute for her. Eventually, they just hired me instead of her! But that's the way you get ahead, child. Even if you're colored, if you're good enough, you'll get the job. As long as they *need* you, you've got that job.

Meanwhile, I was studying for my master's degree in education at Columbia, which I completed in 1925. I was a busy gal, but I was happy being busy. My classes were usually very demanding because as a colored teacher, I always got the meanest kids. Except once.

[3] homemaking skills such as cooking and sewing

That was the year they had me mixed up with a white woman whose name also was Delany. It was kind of funny. She was just furious, because she got all these tough girls, and I got the easy ones—college-bound and motivated. Tell you the truth, I did not mind the tough kids. I loved them all.

It was lonely being about the only colored teacher around. Sometimes the white teachers were friendly, but you couldn't count on any of them being your real friends. There was one woman I was friendly with, and we decided to meet on a Saturday and go swimming at a public pool in the Bronx. I remember that when she saw me in my bathing suit, she looked at my legs and said, "Why, Sarah, you are very white!" And I said, "So what?" I guess she was surprised that I didn't try to pass for white.

Personally, I never had any desire to be white. I am absolutely comfortable with who I am. I used to laugh at how both races seem to hate their hair. All these Negro ladies would run out and get their hair *straightened*, and all these white ladies would run out and get their hair *curled*. My hair was in-between, with a little kink in it, just enough to give it body. I had no desire to change it. I had no desire to change me. I guess I owe that to my Mama and Papa.

This same teacher who seemed to wonder why I didn't just try to "pass" turned out to be a fair-weather friend. Once, she and I had planned to go swimming, and she said to wait under the clock at noon, and so I did. But coincidentally, some other white girls she knew showed up right when she arrived. So she just snubbed me. She didn't want them to know we were friends, so she left me standing there and walked on past, with them. She was so obvious that there really wasn't anything to do but laugh it off and forget about it.

I remained on friendly terms with that woman. Bessie says, "I wouldn't have had nothing more to do with her this side of Glory!" This is the kind of thing that drives Bessie wild. Bessie would have given her a piece of her mind. Sure, it annoyed me. But I didn't let it ruin my day. Life is short, and it's up to you to make it sweet.

About the Author

Sarah Delany and her sister A. Elizabeth Delany (Bessie) dictated *Having Our Say*, the story of their lives, to Amy Hill Hearth when both were over 100 years old. The book tells about the wonderful family life of these remarkable women during a time in our history when African Americans suffered many injustices. "Around Brick Walls" is an excerpt from the book, which has recently been adapted for the stage.

Responding to the Autobiography

▼ Think Back

How did Sarah Delany trick the local board of education into hiring her for a high school teaching position?

How does Sarah feel about her African American roots and the prejudice that has been directed at her?

Why was Sarah's white teacher friend surprised that Sarah didn't try to pass for white?

▼ Discuss

Do you agree with the way in which Sarah Delany got the teaching job? Why or why not?

The Delany sisters disagree about how to handle prejudiced people. Sarah stayed on good terms with her "fair-weather friend," while Bessie says, "I wouldn't have had nothing more to do with her this side of Glory!" Who's right? Why?

▼ Write

Plan an Interview Imagine that you are a student reporter at Theodore Roosevelt High School. You have been assigned to interview the new teacher, Miss Delany. Write a list of at least five questions to ask.

Write an Essay Think about an accomplishment you're proud of. What problems did you overcome? Describe your accomplishment in a style similar to Sarah Delany's.

Theme Links

American History

In this unit, you've read selections about Americans who lived in the past and learned about important historical events that affected their lives. You've also explored how important events change history.

▼ Group Discussion

With a partner or in a small group, talk about the selections in this unit and how they relate to the theme and to your own lives. Use questions like the following to guide the discussion.

- What obstacles did the people or characters in the selections face?
- Do you think life was easier or more difficult in the past? Explain.
- A famous saying argues that history is bound to repeat itself. Do you agree or disagree? Explain.

▼ Imaginary Conversation

Imagine a conversation between Major Sullivan Ballou and 1st Lt. Sharon A. Lane. What would they talk about? With a classmate, role-play a conversation between Ballou and Lane.

▼ Creating a Time Capsule

What do you think future historians will say about the era in which you live? How will they know what your life and your society was like? In a small group, plan what you'd like students in the future to know about your class. Then create a time capsule containing objects that will show students in the future what your class was like. Objects you might put in the time capsule include

- CDs, audiotapes, or videotapes
- current magazines, newspapers, and books
- popular toys
- pictures of famous Americans
- brief essays describing your concerns, hopes, dreams, and achievements as a student.

Write a brief note to accompany each item in the time capsule and explain its significance. Leave instructions in the classroom explaining where you've put the time capsule and when it should be opened. In your instructions, encourage the future class to continue the time capsule tradition by creating one of their own.

▼ The Theme and You

What do you know about your own family history? What experiences did your parents or grandparents have? Does someone in your neighborhood have a story to tell?

Interview an older person. Ask questions about experiences they've had. Take notes. Write an account of something that happened to that person in the past. If possible, make an audiotape or videotape of your subject telling about her or his life.

Acknowledgments

Acknowledgment is gratefully made to the following publishers, authors, and agents for permission to reprint these works. Every effort has been made to determine copyright owners. In the case of any omissions, the Publisher will be pleased to make suitable acknowledgments in future editions.

"When I Hear Your Name" by Gloria Fuertes from *Off the Map* © 1984 by Gloria Fuertes and Wesleyan University Press. By permission of University Press of New England.

"The Good Stuff" from *It Was On Fire When I Lay Down On It* by Robert Fulghum. Copyright © 1988, 1989 by Robert Fulghum. Reprinted by permission of Villard Books, a division of Random House, Inc.

"Los Ancianos" by Pat Mora is reprinted with permission from the publisher of *Borders* (Houston: Arte Público Press–University of Houston, 1986).

"Mark Messner" by Mitch Albom, from *Best Sports Stories*. Copyright © 1989. Reprinted by permission of Detroit Free Press.

"Mother" by Bea Exner Liu. Originally published by Milkweed Editions. Reprinted by permission of the author.

"The Night We Started Dancing" by Ann Cameron from *Free To Be . . . A Family*, Free To Be Foundation, Inc., Conceived by Marlo Thomas, Copyright 1987. Reprinted by permission.

"Grandma Traub" and "Grandma Ling" from *Chinamerican Reflections, Poems and Paintings* by Amy Ling. Lewiston, ME: Great Raven Press, 1984. Used with permission of the author.

"The Education of a Woman Golfer" from *The Education of a Woman Golfer* by Nancy Lopez. Reprinted by permission of IMG Literary. Copyright 1979 by Nancy Lopez.

"Grassy's Theme" by Jesse Stuart reprinted from *Today's Education*, the National Education Association Journal, December 1965, © 1965 by the National Education Association.

"Martin Luther King Jr." by Gwendolyn Brooks. Reprinted by permission of Broadside Press.

"Opera, Karate, and Bandits" from *The Land I Lost: Adventures of A Boy In Vietnam* by Huynh Quang Nhuong. Text copyright 1982 by Huynh Quang Nhuong. Reprinted by permission of HarperCollins College Publishers.